Secret Wisdom

A Nest Egg Of Wisdom That Will Direct Your
Journey Through Life.

Ruby Fleurcius

Secret Wisdom

A Nest Egg Of Wisdom That Will Direct Your Journey Through Life.

Spiritually Fit Publications
Ruby Fleurcius
581 N. Park Ave. Ste. #725
Apopka, FL 32704
321-312-0744

Published in the United States of America

ISBN: 978-0983207566
$14.95

Table of Contents

DEDICATION

I would like to dedicate this book to all of those who are seeking to understand the hidden truths about wisdom. We envision the perfect fairytale life, and I wish that for everyone as well; but, what do we do when it becomes a living nightmare? What then? Hopefully, that is not the case; but, it is you that I dedicate this book to. I am reaching into the depths of my soul to pull out hope and restoration for you; I have been where you are. I was once blind to reality, not because I could not see; it was that I did not want to see. I could not bear the pain of my little empire crashing down if I opened my eyes—until that one day came that I had to stop lying to myself. I had to stop lying to life, I had to stop lying to God, I had to begin to own my life, I had to begin to learn the types of people that I needed to avoid in order to protect my sanity, and I needed to learn how to listen to the VOICE from within. My inner-born wisdom began to speak louder than anyone I knew when I learned the secrets of how to listen to it.

As it began to guide me through life—I have become an expert on repeating back what the Voice speaks to me.

I am constantly asked questions about my quotes or the source of my information; therefore, I am going to answer this question publically. I write randomly, I write from experience, I write out of revelation, I write out of inspiration, I write out of obedience, and I write from within....I do not write in vain or just to spill my guts; I write because that is my God-given mission, as well as my God-given talent. When I write, I hold nothing back—I give it to you the way it is spiritually uttered to me. Most often, I have people thinking that I am sending them a silent message through what I write; however, that may or may not be true at all—I write what I am given; and, if the shoe fits, wear it! The way in which I write is my LEGACY......it's not a message to one person......it is Divine Inspiration of Healing that's designed to outlive me.

Now, as the wailing of your soul calleth the deep unto deep, let the greatness from within take its rightful place in your life. No matter how it seems, it's your moment in time to embrace the "Secret Wisdom" from within. To God be the Glory. Amen.

INTRODUCTION

This book, **"Secret Wisdom"** is going to reveal some of the Hidden Secrets of the Bible that are designed to help you trust God for Divine Provision.   Of course, you may very well be able to provide for your own daily needs physically; but, what about your spiritual needs, emotional needs, mental needs, or spiritual guidance?   One is just as important as the other, so why are we neglecting them?   Is God not able to provide for them on a daily basis?   Of course, He is indeed able to provide for those needs, but is it possible that He is withholding provision in those areas of dire need?   I believe that the provisions that you are waiting for are wrapped up in the people, places, and things that you are running from mentally, physically, emotionally, and spiritually.   If you are reading this book, it's time for you to forgive and move on. It is time for you to trust God to open up your destiny enriched provisions to allow your gift to make room for you; therefore, enabling you to find the wisdom to bring forth the TRUTH that's inside of you.

The Book of Proverbs is indeed the ultimate precepts of wisdom known to man.   Although, we may have our doubts about the Bible, but one thing we will find is that the "Secret Wisdom" regarding life principles are hidden deep within the Book of Proverbs. As I follow the leading of the Spirit, Proverbs 3:32 reveals that "His secret counsel is with the upright." Therefore, if we have the desire to become upright, then [She] Wisdom will become our guide, as well as our secret counsel on this unavoidable journey called life.

Our secret counsel, [She] Wisdom, says that if we would like to learn the truth about how to communicate effectively, the truth about our folly, the truth about our slothfulness, the truth about our gossiping, the truth about our slandering, the truth about committing adultery, the truth about our virtues, the truth about our values, or the truth about Godly character, we must search the depths of the hidden wisdom located in the Book of Proverbs. [She] Wisdom, also advises that we must come seeking her, she will not seek us—it is now our responsibility to seek that in which Adam and Eve forfeited in the Garden of Eden.

As life unravels the secrets of the Great Unknown, one secret that we must all know is that a proverb is not just a mere proverb when using the Bible. Let me explain, the Book of Proverbs is where [She] Wisdom meets us to provide the First Secret teachings on how to become a Pro at using our Verbs. As we all know, a verb is an action or state of being located in a sentence or statement. And, according to [She] Wisdom, it is through our actions, positive or negative, that produce our end result. In my opinion, our life is like one big VERB! Our actions speak volumes about our character without us saying one word; and whether we realize it or not, our actions are the focal point of our direction in life.

What I have found is that The Book of Proverbs is indeed the lifeline, or better yet, the life coach to fine-tuning our actions, enabling us to behave like a wise pro, not someone without any home training. It also enables us to learn how to use words to motivate, encourage, build, and shut down when necessary through our actions, reactions, comparisons, and state of being. However, at the end of the day, we are representatives of where and who we came from; therefore, we should allow our ultimate goal to become better than where we came from, not bitter from where we came from.

Although I do not proclaim to be perfect, nor do I proclaim to live a life without flaws; however, throughout my journey, I have found that the Book of Psalms would help me to pray through my issues, and the Book of Proverbs would help me to recognize them; regardless of whether the issues were within me, with someone around me, based on my actions, reactions, or the lack thereof. For these simple heartfelt reasons, I have taken the time to write **"The Ancient Wisdom of Psalms"** to help us use scriptures to pray through our issues, and **"Secret Wisdom"** to help us to recognize the cause of our issues, while guiding us with wise counsel on how to bring a resolve to what we are dealing with, what's dealing with us, or what we refuse to deal with. And, no matter where we are in life, we all have something to deal with, some more than others, but the truth remains that we all have issues. [She] Wisdom is designed to open the curtains to the hidden wisdom that is overlooked every single day through our lack of understanding; therefore, making it okay to take the mask off to be who we truly are.

When our life is in turmoil, it is common to look for a miracle to come from someone else outside of ourselves; but,

I believe that our miracle is within us. We often pray for God to send someone to help us, opposed to praying for God to help us to help ourselves. Better yet, we often pray for God to send us a word or confirmation regarding our situation or circumstance, and He has already given it to us in the Book of Proverbs. He reveals all that we need to know, but for some odd reason, we choose to go by the opinions of others when our answer is right before us in plain sight.

This book entitled, "Secret Wisdom" is extracted from Genesis 22: 1-13 in the Bible, and the entire Book of Proverbs—I will show how the seeds of Abraham produced The Secret Tree of Life. Once we understand that no one is exempt from problems, issues, and losses, we are better able to embrace our faith with an inner knowing that all things will work together for our good. If we look around us right now, we will see that we are blessed; but, for some odd reason, we can't seem to embrace or understand our blessings—so we keep looking around for something or someone that will only keep us feeling aloof, looking for our next quick-fix. Most often the scales on our eyes or our selfishness prevent us from seeing life clearly; therefore, causing our blessings not to appear as blessings or to possibly appear as curses. Although we may know something is there, but we can't seem to get to it, or its appearance may not be appealing to us; and, this is where this book, "Secret Wisdom" comes into play to ensure that we do not overlook the diamond that is in the ruff.

[She] Wisdom will also help you recognize who you are, and why you are, despite how far your back is up against the wall regarding the people, places, and things in your life. It is my reasonable service as a child of the Most High, to allow [She] Wisdom to speak through me to reveal some of the secrets to obtaining the provisions for the next step in your life; or, to simply help you to understand The Secret Tree of Life that is already hidden right in your own backyard! You have what you need, let us help you find it, let us help you own it, let us help you diligently build the desires of your heart, as we unriddle the great wisdom that's hidden in plain sight to ensure that you are able to get out of your own way.

Take it from me; it is not good to surround ourselves with people, places, and things that are always tearing our kingdom down—if we want all that God has to offer us; we need to surround ourselves with KINGDOM BUILDERS who are not ashamed to build their lives one brick at a time. From this point on, I need you to get from under the bus, and pick up a brick—it's time to start rebuilding the Empire that's already hidden inside of you.

CHAPTER 1

The Mind-Germ

Life is definitely what we make of it; but, more importantly, our life is our seed, and it will become a guide to us if we allow it to do so. Choices come, and choices go; bottom line, we choose our own path at some point in our lives. It is our choices that become the fertilizer for the seeds that are planted within us, positively or negatively. Now, the question is, "After the seed of childhood, then what?" We take over with the tools that we are given during our upbringing, and whatever we do not have by then, we must make a choice to get it, learn it, improvise, negotiate, or do without. Nevertheless, whatever we did or did not receive during childhood, we will still have some form of longing from within. Basically, it's a longing for more than what we have right now, a longing for what we think that we did not receive, a longing to be who we are not, a longing for something. If we do not fill that longing with the right thing, "IT" will grow; therefore, causing us to become vulnerable to the mind-germs that fill that longing for that

"IT!" What do I mean by that "IT?" I mean that longing, that emptiness, that void, that "IT" that we cannot tell anyone about. That "IT" that's revealed in our actions, that "IT" that's revealed in our reactions, that "IT" that's revealed in our thoughts, that "IT" that's revealed in our decisions, that "IT" that's revealed in our quest for freedom, or that "IT" that's revealed in our desire to read this book right now.

In dealing with life on a daily basis, I would like to keep it simple; but, you and I know that it's not that simple; especially when dealing with people outside of our circle, the people that we are unequally yoked with, or the people that are stuck on negative. Therefore, in order to excel to the next level, or prevent ourselves from falling into the ruts of negativity, we must begin to learn and understand some of the Godly characteristics that are required to become truly wise in dealing with self, the woes of life, as well as dealing with difficult people. Now, what I have found is that the Book of Proverbs written primarily by King Solomon helps us with this tedious task of learning the characteristics of a wise person and a fool. I am not referring to anyone as a fool, or calling anyone names, I am only referring to the foolish behavior of the unwise to give a better understanding of where we are, where we are going, how we are going to get there, who's going to help us, and who we are going to help along the way.

King Solomon and many other writers in the Book of Proverbs left us a fortress of wisdom for us to follow, and for some odd reason, it's constantly overlooked by those who are desperately seeking help in certain areas of weakness. However, before I go into the background of

King Solomon, let me preface this with how it all got started with a sacrifice. We can consider it a cost, price, or sacrifice; it's all the same in my opinion. If we think that we can free-load off of life, we are sadly mistaken—we must apply ourselves in some way, shape, or form. In so many words, life will ask something of us; and, we must decide if we are going to make the sacrifice to obtain it.

I know this book is about "Secret Wisdom", but I do want to preface it with a biblical story of where Abraham was promised a son by God, and after a long period of drought and waiting, He finally gave him a son, only to ask him to sacrifice his seed many years later. In Genesis 22: 1-18, *Now it came to pass after these things that God tested Abraham, and said to him, "Abraham!" And he said, "Here I am." Then He said, "Take now your son, your only son Isaac, whom you love, and go to the land of Moriah, and offer him there as a burnt-offering on one of the mountains of which I shall tell you." So Abraham rose early in the morning and saddled his donkey, and took two of his young men with him, and Isaac his son; and he split the wood for the burnt offering, and arose and went to the place of which God had told him. Then on the third day Abraham lifted his eyes and saw the place afar off. And Abraham said to his young men, "Stay here with the donkey; the lad and I will go yonder and worship, and we will come back to you." So Abraham took the wood of the burnt offering and laid it on Isaac his son; and he took the fire in his hand, and a knife, and the two of them went together. But Isaac spoke to Abraham his father and said, "My father!" And he said, "Here I am, my son." Then he said, "Look, the fire and the wood, but where is the lamb for a burnt offering?" And Abraham said, "My son, God will provide for Himself the lamb for a burnt offering." So the two of them went together. Then they came to the place of which God had told him. And*

Abraham built an altar there and placed the wood in order; and he bound Isaac his son and laid him on the altar, upon the wood. And Abraham stretched out his hand and took the knife to slay his son. But the Angel of the Lord called to him from heaven and said, "Abraham, Abraham!" So he said, "Here I am." And He said, "Do not lay your hand on the lad, or do anything to him; for now I know that you fear God, since you have not withheld your son, your only son, from Me." Then Abraham lifted his eyes and looked, and there behind him was a ram caught in a thicket by its horns. So Abraham went and took the ram, and offered it up for a burnt-offering instead of his son. And Abraham called the name of the place, The-Lord-Will-Provide; as it is said to this day, "In the Mount of the Lord it shall be provided." Then the Angel of the Lord called to Abraham a second time out of heaven, and said: "By Myself I have sworn, says the Lord, because you have done this thing, and have not withheld your son, your only son—blessing I will bless you, and multiplying I will multiply your descendants as the stars of the heaven and as the sand which is on the seashore; and your descendants shall possess the gate of their enemies. In your seed all the nations of the earth shall be blessed, because you have obeyed My voice."

It is because of Abraham that we are entitled to reap the rewards of his faithfulness and positive attitude. Therefore, in my opinion, it is only wise that we uphold the same principles, standards, and ethics of the one who opened the door for our entitlement. Better yet, as we speak about entitlement, it is through King Solomon, the son of King David, and the Seed of Abraham that [She] Wisdom allowed the (Wisdom of God) to be put on paper, to ensure that we can glean the "Secret Wisdom" of our Spiritual Priesthood. In so many words, if we desire to become wise like Kings, Queens, or the Elite, we must begin to think like them, and the most profound way to do so is to begin to understand what [She] Wisdom has hidden in the pages of Proverbs. Nevertheless, before we begin, it is imperative that we get an understanding of an Oracle. Most often we think of an Oracle as a mystical type of person, but in all actuality, an Oracle is a word, message; or a response from a Higher Source. Hopefully, that Higher Source would be Our Father, which art in Heaven, but that is not always the case with everyone because we do have the potential of manipulating religion to cater to what we want or are trained to believe. Now, here is how it works, God does use certain individuals to spread the message, give a word, or bring about revelation on certain things; and, He will use our lives as an Oracle to spread His word, which is often called our Testimony. In my opinion, we are all Oracles of Life; we were spoken into existence with one word. So, are we not a Word of God? Are we not an Oracle of God? Are we not created in His image? The answer is "Yes" we are an Oracle that is created in His image—if we are a living being, we all have a Spirit, we all have intuition, and we all have a message to leave behind. However, to get back to that state of being—it is going to take some work, and that is where [She] Wisdom steps in as the Oracle to guide us back to our rightful place to not only hear the Voice of God but to become the Voice as well.

When striking up conversations regarding life in general, I often get the question, "Why is our worth not recognized by others?" In my opinion, this could happen for many different reasons, but the most common reasons would be that we do not recognize our own worth, people have lost faith in our worthiness, we are too emotional, we are carrying too much baggage, we are an undercover hypocrite, or we lack wisdom in what we are doing, saying, and becoming. For that reason, according to Proverbs 1:2-6, it lays down simple instructions about proverbial wisdom to prevent us from questioning our worthiness, it says *"To know wisdom and instruction; to perceive the words of understanding; To receive the instruction of wisdom, justice, and judgment, and equity; To give subtilty to the simple, to the young man knowledge and discretion. A wise man will hear, and will increase learning; and a man of understanding shall attain unto wise counsels: To understand a proverb, and the interpretation; the words of the wise, and their dark sayings. The fear of the Lord is the beginning of knowledge; fools despise wisdom and their riddles."*

When we do not follow instructions, when we develop a deaf ear to people, and when we are not true to ourselves, we know it, and others can see it; regardless of how we try to cover it up. We must always remember that our credibility is wrapped up in the things that we say, as well as the things that we don't say. Rest assured that lip service means nothing if action is not taking place; and, for me, the quickest way to lose credibility is to make empty promises or to become unstable in all your ways. I am sure that I am not the only one that feels that way because Proverbs 4:6 tells us to *give careful thought to the paths for our feet and be steadfast in all our ways.*

Believability and trust are indeed the vital ingredients that hold our credibility together, and once our credibility is ruined, it will become hard for people to trust what comes out of our mouth. This is why King Solomon tells us in Proverbs 23:23 to *buy the truth, and sell it not; also wisdom, and instruction, and understanding.* The value of our words is our bond; therefore, *get wisdom, get understanding: forget it not; neither decline from the words of my mouth.* In so many words, our actions must line up with what we know, and what we know must begin to line up with our actions, because we cannot speak about foolishness and expect wisdom to flow out of the same gateway. Yes, there is a time and place for everything; however, foolish behavior gives room for folly, and we cannot expect to stay on top of our game when we are busy playing mind games with the people, places and things we love. If we are convinced that we are worthy of something or someone, we do not have to try too hard to show off. All we have to do is simply walk in it, exercise faith, wisdom, understanding, integrity, and due diligence, for Proverbs 18:16 clearly states that *"a man's gift maketh room for him, and bringeth him before great men."*

When we know what we want, and have scriptures to back it up while increasing our knowledge daily to get it—we remove our own limits; therefore, defeating the sluggard mentality that causes divine wisdom to elude us. Proverbs 13:4 says that *"The soul of the sluggard craves and gets nothing, but the soul of the diligent is made fat."* Today, take a moment to line up your actions and get busy building, creating, doing, and becoming. The pauper mentality is not a desired trait that is conducive to the teachings of King Solomon, nor was it the instructions given to him by his mother. His mother taught him the proverbial instructions of his father, King David, the writer of Psalms, many years before he assumed his role as king. Therefore, he was rooted and grounded in the "Secret Wisdom" of his forefathers at a young age, giving him the upper hand in leading his field.

Whether you have stopped believing in you, whether people have stopped believing in you, or whether you have become lost in the pains, the trials, or the chaos of life, you must look from within for your strength, because *happy is the man that finds wisdom, and the man that gets understanding.*

Is it possible that our attitude, our actions, or our behavior on the outside of our house affect what takes place on the inside of our house? The answer is a quick YES for me. The Law of Reciprocity is in high effect, do not think for a minute that we can behave badly and expect peace as a result—that's not going to happen. When chaos and confusion are running rampant, we must find peace in the midst of it; according to scripture, *"He that hath no rule over his own spirit is like a city that is broken down, and without walls."* Proverbs 25:28. We cannot allow the things that are taking place around us to cause us to lose our temper or lack the self-control needed to think rationally. In my opinion, we have a lot more at stake; therefore, we must think wisely before reacting because it may affect the innocent people that we love or affect the innocent people that we know nothing about. As we all are aware that anything can happen at any given moment; therefore, we must keep our wits about us at all times. However, I will say this, violence is not the answer! According to Proverbs 16:29, *"Violent people deceive their friends and lead them to disaster."* And, if we do not become mentally and emotionally strong about the things that are taking place around us, we will become consumed with the perplexities that are trying to keep us bound. Remember, there is nothing new under the sun, and it's through wisdom that our house is built; and it's through love, joy, peace, kindness, goodness, faithfulness, gentleness, and self-control that it is established. This will keep the **MIND CONTROL GERM** from turning one person against another to create division among us. Take it from me, *"He that is slow to anger is better than the mighty; and he* *that ruleth his spirit than he that taketh a city."* Proverbs 16:32. Your strength and peace reside in loving and respecting all humanity regardless of creed or deed; because if you do not, true value cannot be found in the people, places, and things you hate. Lastly, exhibiting hatefulness in your actions, reactions, or spoken words will cause the true essence of a peaceful life to elude the place in which hate resides; therefore, love thy neighbor as you love thyself.

CHAPTER 2

Our Secret Investments

Everyone has a secret! Believe it or not, it is the secrets that are unknown to all that sparks our curiosity to know more of what we did not know before. I would call it a little edge, some would call it the scoop, and some will simply call it classified information. Regardless of what we call our secrets—revealing inside information is exactly why the news media, social media, and gossip columns make tons of money. In my opinion, if we take the time to learn a few secrets, we may as well make it beneficial. If the secrets that are being revealed to us are not taking us to the next level in life, then we must exercise caution regarding our participation in such behavior.

Now, the *Second Secret of Proverbs* that I will reveal is that you are the Seed of Abraham, and you have the right to lay claim to your inheritance. Let me explain, in Genesis, Chapter 15—God promised that He would bless Abraham, make him a great nation, and bless the nation as well; and you are a part of that promise. But, the promise comes with conditions—God did not tell Abraham that the blessings would just fall into his lap—he and his descendants had to work for them. Although the covenant is everlasting, Abraham and his descendants were required to hold up their part of the covenant; and that was to pray to only Him, worship Him, listen to Him, obey Him, and to follow His will. However, in following all the rules, there was still something lacking, and that was Godly wisdom. *According to 1 Kings 3:5-14, "At Gibeon the Lord appeared to Solomon in a dream by night; and God said, "Ask! What shall I give you?" And Solomon said: "You have shown great mercy to Your servant David my father, because he walked before You in truth, in righteousness, and in uprightness of heart with You; You have continued this great kindness for him, and You have given him a son to sit on his throne, as it is this day. Now, O 'Lord my God, You have made Your servant king instead of my father David, but I am a little child; I do not know how to go out or come in. And Your servant is in the midst of Your people whom You have chosen, a great people, too numerous to be numbered or counted. Therefore give to Your servant an understanding heart to judge Your people, that I may discern between good and evil. For who is able to judge this great people of Yours?" The speech pleased the Lord, that Solomon had asked this thing. Then God said to him: "Because you have asked this thing, and have not asked long life for yourself, nor have asked riches for yourself, nor have asked the life of your enemies, but have asked for yourself understanding to discern justice, behold, I have done according to your words; see, I have given you a wise and understanding heart, so that there has not been anyone like you before you, nor shall any like you arise after you. And I have also given you what you have not asked: both riches and honor, so that there shall not be anyone like you among the kings all your days. So if you walk in My ways, to keep My statutes and My commandments, as your father David walked, then I will lengthen your days."* As a result, King Solomon put together several proverbs to guide us in practical wisdom regarding life skills to safeguard our blessings, to prevent us from cursing our own hand, and to bring structure into our lives. As his legacy lives on, the same wisdom that he asked for, is available to each and every one of us, we only need to ask and follow instructions. The voice of wisdom says in Proverbs 8:1-4, *"Does not wisdom cry out, And understanding lift up her voice? She takes her stand on the top of the high hill, beside the way, where the paths meet. She cries out by the gates, at the entry of the city, at the entrance of the doors: "To you, O men, I call."* Wisdom is calling out to you, why will you not answer? [She] Wisdom awaits your call...................

What is so sacred about wisdom? And, what is the big hype about? Divine wisdom is from God, and human wisdom is considered carnal because it's based solely upon human reasoning or conditioning. In my opinion, human wisdom is not exactly wisdom; I simply call it a good decision or good judgment. Regardless of how we see wisdom, there is no comparison to the wisdom that flows from God, there is no comparison to instinctual wisdom, and there is no comparison to the wisdom of the Holy Spirit. Wisdom says in Proverbs 8:6-11 that *"I will speak of excellent things, and from the opening of my lips will come right things; for my mouth will speak truth; wickedness is an abomination to my lips. All the words of my mouth are with righteousness; nothing crooked or perverse is in them. They are all plain to him who understands, and right to those who find knowledge. Receive my instruction, and not silver, And knowledge rather than choice gold; for wisdom is better than rubies, and all the things one may desire cannot be compared with her."* We cannot go wrong using practical wisdom. Trust me, when all else fails, [She] Wisdom, will not!

It doesn't matter how we may or may not feel about reading the Bible, but there are indeed hidden truths that ungodly individuals have mastered to outsmart Godly individuals. I am not here to judge who exhibits Godly characteristics and who does not, my goal is to empower willing vessels with the *"Secrets to the Tree of Life."* Now, with that in mind, the *Third Secret of Proverbs* is that we are blessed until our actions, reactions, thoughts, or demeanor proves otherwise. In so many words, we are born with a silver spoon in our mouth; we are entitled to what we believe we are entitled to—if we believe that we are blessed, then we are; basically, we become what we think about all the time. On the other hand, if we believe that we are cursed, then our perception of known and unknown curses will begin to permeate our lives with or without our permission because that is what we actually believe. However, there are certain people, places, and things that the *Book of Proverbs* heeds great warning against; and, there are certain actions, reactions, thoughts, and behaviors that we must possess in order to truly understand the *Secret Wisdom of God.*

When we glean from the mind of a Ruler, we must take into account that this type of information is not for everyone; however, wisdom is supreme, and it's **available** to everyone—[She] Wisdom says that *"I love those who love me, and those who seek me diligently will find me"* (*Proverbs 8:17*). For this reason, **"Secret Wisdom"** helps to make understanding the *Book of Proverbs* easy for the elite, as well as the average person who is seeking more out of life than what they are getting. And, one thing that I know personally is that *"wisdom is better*

Chapter 2 | Ruby Fleurcius

than rubies, and all the things one may desire cannot be compared with her" (Proverbs 8:11). I cannot place a price tag on the wisdom that God has bestowed upon me to uncover some of the *Hidden Secrets of Proverbs.*

As life progresses with or without us, the wisdom that is hidden in Proverbs has an insurmountable treasure chest of benefits that are designed to teach us the Spiritual way of getting what we want without creating enemies along the way. Here are some of the learnable benefits that are available to you in *The Book of Proverbs:*

Learn the fear of God.
Learn wisdom and discipline.
Learn the value of understanding.
Learn how to receive and obey instructions.
Learn how to deal with life lessons.
Learn how to value knowledge.
Learn how to exercise discretion.
Learn why we need to exercise prudence.
Learn how to embrace wise counsel.
Learn how to treat people.
Learn the value of respect.
Learn the importance of humility.
Learn who to hang out with or who to avoid.
Learn how to develop Godly character.
Learn how to treat your parents or your elders.
Learn about the rod of correction.

How can we really invest in ourselves, or build *The Tree of life* from within, when we have nothing to give or sacrifice? I have been faced with this same question time and time again—what I have found is that we all have something to give to ourselves, and that is our TIME! The way in which we invest our time with ourselves will determine our level of commitment. If we feel as if we cannot be alone, or do things on our own, that is a tell-tell sign that we need to invest more time into self. In my opinion, it is the inner-self that's going to keep us afloat in our time of need; therefore, preventing co-dependency from creeping in, causing us to do things that we would not ordinarily do. Yes, we can say that we have self-control; but, until it is tried and tested—it means nothing. It is through the testing phases of our life that our level of commitment shows up to bail us out. However, if we have not invested in the building of our inner-self, it is possible that we may crash & burn in our most eminent time of need. No, I do not wish doom & gloom on anyone, but this is a reality check—there is a time and a season for everything under the sun. Therefore, in our time of harvest, we must store up for our time of famine for that is the inevitable.

I certainly am a big believer in destiny, because I am living proof of it. There are many different paths that will get us to our destination, and we must choose one. We can take the long way, the short way, or the wrong way—it's our choice. As we all know Newton's third law: "For every action, there is an equal or opposite reaction." In my opinion, every move we make in life must be well calculated, or it may work against us. I am not saying that we must overthink issues, circumstances, or events that take place in our lives—I am saying that we must think through them to ensure that distractions are kept to a bare minimum. When we make decisions with this principle in mind, it will ensure that we do not fall victim to instant gratification that leads us in the wrong direction. As we look back over our lives, where we are now, is a byproduct of the choices that we have made, and nothing will change unless we do.

As long as the earth rotates on its axis, people will see us three ways: 1. They will see us how we see ourselves. 2. They will see us how they see themselves. 3. They will see the truth about who we are without being biased in their perception. Now, what really matters is how we see ourselves, and until we understand and acknowledge the truth about who we are and why we are here, we will become aloof when people express how they feel, or what they think about us; therefore, contributing to our bad attitude or our antisocialism. We are who we are, and there is nothing wrong with fine-tuning our ability to have a pleasant experience when we come in contact with others, or for others to have a pleasant experience in our presence. The truth is that we are in control of who we are, and that should be our main focus. Regardless of what others think, do, or say, it is our responsibility to make a positive impact on the lives of others—a simple smile, a word of encouragement, a helping hand, a thank-you, etc. will make a difference.

If you want to begin to reap the benefits of the *Tree of Life*, you must begin to find a way to stop groaning, whining, and complaining about what people did not do for you, what people did to you, or how people treated you; because, if you are reading this book right now, it does not matter anyway. Your entitlement from this point forward will be governed by your ATTITUDE. So with that being said, pay it forward with the right attitude, while investing in your inner-self;

because what's inside of you will show up when you are squeezed to the max. From me to you, never stop learning— you are an open book that's bound to be read at some point in time.

Our Investments in life will determine who we are or who we will become, positively or negatively. Nevertheless, when there is a lack of investment in what we should invest in—it will become noticeable physically, mentally, emotionally, spiritually, or financially, especially when there is some form of neglect taking place. In my opinion, we receive back what we put in; for example, our mind—we will receive back what we put into it. Another example, our body, we will get back what we put into it. Our finances, we will get back what we put in. If we are lazy about our investments, then our investments will not be obligated to give us a return.

In the Bible, it speaks about training up a child in the way that they should go, and when they grow old, they will never depart from it. Most often, we think that scripture is only referring to a child; however, in my opinion, it is applicable to every area of our lives. Anything or anyone that we are nurturing applies to this principle—our personal hygiene for example, it's not a child, but if we do not take care of ourselves—it will become noticeable. Our mind, our body, our soul, our spirit, our well-being, our family, and our finances are all investments; therefore, it is imperative that we groom those areas appropriately. As a matter of fact, even if we do not get the desired results on something or someone that we are investing in; rest assured, based on the principle of seed, time, and harvest, it will bear fruit in due season. Oh, by the way, this works both positively and negatively; therefore, it is best to always stay on the positive end of the spectrum. In my opinion, there is no need to sacrifice your soul, when all you have to do is INVEST in it. Your purpose is designed to serve you as soon as you realize its value, exercise GODLY characteristics, and operate in the spirit of excellence with outright integrity in all that you do.

CHAPTER 3

The Power of Taking Risks

As we look around, we have all different types of trees around us, yet there is one that's in plain sight that eludes us; and, that is the *Tree of Life.* Okay, let me get a little biblical for a minute, in Genesis 2:8 it says, *"The Lord God planted a garden eastward in Eden, and there He put the man whom He had formed. And out of the ground the Lord God made every tree grow that is pleasant to the sight and good for food. The tree of life was also in the midst of the garden, and the tree of the knowledge of good and evil."* And, according to Genesis 2:5-7, *Then the Lord God took the man and put him in the Garden of Eden to tend and keep it. And the Lord God commanded the man, saying, "Of every tree of the garden you may freely eat; but of the tree of the knowledge of good and evil you shall not eat, for in the day that you eat of it you shall surely die."* After the partaking of the forbidden fruit by Adam and Eve from the *Tree of Good and Evil,* their eyes were opened to the real world; or better yet, life as we have it today. We are living the continuation of the curse of disobedience in our day to day lives by having to work hard and suffer for everything that we have. We sometimes suffer in a good way, and sometimes we suffer in a bad way; however, we do not have to become bound by our suffering, because we have the *Tree of Life* left. After that one act of disobedience, God has hidden the *Tree of Life* in plain sight, which means that if we are not ready to see it, we will not see it no matter how hard we try!

Nevertheless, for those who are willing, I have found that the *Tree of Life* is written all over The Book of Proverbs. Take a look:

- *She [wisdom] is a tree of life to those who take hold of her, and happy are all who retain her.* Proverbs 3:18
- *The fruit of the righteous is a tree of life, and he who wins souls is wise.* Proverbs 11:30
- *Hope deferred makes the heart sick, but when the desire comes, it is a tree of life.* Proverbs 13:12
- *A wholesome tongue is a tree of life but perverseness in it breaks the spirit.* Proverbs 15:4

Although we are blessed, the afflictions of life have enough power to make us doubt what we actually believe—so much so that we wallow in self-pity. Of course, it has happened to the best of us, and if this has not happened at some point in our lives, just live a little longer—life does have a way of squeezing us until our tree breaks or produce. In my opinion, we cannot get the oil out of the olive unless we squeeze it; or better yet, we cannot enjoy orange juice, if the orange is not squeezed. Most often, our blessing will not reveal itself until we are squeezed, tried, rooted, grounded, and tested. Although we may be entitled to it, it does not mean that we are going to obtain it without working for it.

Why do we have to pay for the sins of Adam and Eve? It is not a matter of paying for the sins of another; it's a matter of living through the sins of our forefathers. Which brings us to the *Fourth Secret of Proverbs* is that we are a representative of where we came from to safeguard our family's good name. In so many words, *"A good name is to be more desired than great wealth, favor is better than silver and gold."* Proverbs 22:1, because *"The name of the righteous is used in blessings, but the name of the wicked will rot."* Proverbs 10:7. We cannot behave badly, and think for a minute that we will get away with our behavioral mishaps. Uncorrected behavioral mishaps create a generational curse that produces an excess amount of rotten fruit that will fall from our *Tree of Good and Evil*. The sins of a mother or the sins of a father will pass down to his or her seed; however, the impact will depend upon our ability to repent, our ability to pray, our ability to ask for forgiveness, our ability to ask for mercy, and our ability to plead the Blood of Jesus over our offspring. If we do not repent, we will find that our offspring will repeat the same acts of sin only with a different mask, along with a generational curse attached to it.

To safeguard our good name, we must avail ourselves, as well as our offspring to the *Tree of Life* located in the *Book of Proverbs* as early as possible. This is what [She] Wisdom nudged King Solomon to tell us: *"Train up a child in the way he should go, and when he is old he will not depart from it."* Proverbs 22:6. Although, kids will be kids, and no one is perfect; however, our children are a blessing from God, but it's our responsibility to represent a good name and teach our children the value of having a good name as well. [She] Wisdom advises us that *"He who spares his rod hates his son, but* he who loves him disciplines him promptly." Proverbs 13:24; and that "A fool rejects his father's discipline, but he who regards reproof is prudent." Proverbs 15:5. From my personal experiences, scriptural truths can and will change our lives for the better regardless of where we came from if we allow correction, teaching, rebuking, training, and a lot of love to nurture the good and bad that's hidden in all of us. Always keep in mind that the actions that we take today may affect our seeds of tomorrow.

What is the determining factor that governs where we came from or a good name? Our attitude determines everything. Our attitude is the one thing that we cannot run away from—it is like our shadow, it will follow us everywhere, and when illuminated from the appropriate direction, it will show up, guaranteed. Make no mistake about it, it is true that our attitudes can indeed make us or break us; or better yet, our attitude can take us places where mere charm cannot. In my opinion, it is very disheartening to have an attractive person become very ugly because of their attitude—when our attitude should be the icing on the cake to get and keep the people, places, and things that we so desire. Regardless of whether we feel attractive or not, our attitude will become the determining factor of how we live our lives, as well as what will live within us that will be governed by the seeds that we have sown. Trust me, everything that we may feel that we are not; it is our attitude that bridges the gap or burns down bridges.

We are surrounded by all types of attitudes, and it is also the contributing factor of what makes us or what breaks us in this place we call the REAL WORLD. Our code of conduct rules for us or against us without our permission because everything that we do, say, or become is a derivative of our five senses of Seeing, Hearing, Touching, Smelling, and Tasting; therefore, making everything emotionally, mentally, physically, or spiritually personable. In so many words, we are driven emotionally, mentally, physically, and spiritually by our five senses whether we like it or not! Our attitude will tell us everything that our mouth is not bold enough to say, as well as the hidden secrets or issues of the heart; therefore, we must, *"Watch over our heart with all diligence, for from it flows the springs of life."* Proverbs 4:3. This would only leave one to ask, "How could something so profound, such as our attitude become so misunderstood?" I would say that it is the trick of the enemy to set ourselves up for our own defeat through the one thing that the real world sees without us saying one word. For this reason, the Bible tells us to *"Let this mind be in you which was also in Christ Jesus,"* Philippians 1:27. Therefore, giving us the opportunity to lead by example or become a positive role-model setting forth a good name of where we came from.

As life unravels, it is our attitude that separates the boys from gentlemen and the girls from ladies. It is said in scripture that *"When I was a child, I spoke as a child, I understood as a child, I thought as a child; but when I became a man, I put away childish things."* 1 Corinthians 13:11. Of course, we can rationalize and justify our womanhood or manhood, but life has a way of putting us in categories based on the choices that we make for ourselves. And just because we have crossed over into adulthood physically does not mean that we have crossed over emotionally, mentally, or spiritually. Most often, as we focus on outer growth, we tend to forget about the growth that takes place on the inside of us. Unfortunately, if the inner growth is forgotten about, it could become devastating to the management and the accountability of everyday life regardless of our age. That's why Proverbs 9:9 tells us to *"Give instruction to a wise man and he will be still wiser, teach a righteous man and he will increase his learning."*

As time continues, our attitude has become the silent killer of those who refuse to understand that a good name is to be chosen. Personally, a lackadaisical attitude is the playground of negativity and misunderstanding that reproduces the victim mentality without the individual knowing what's happening to them. *"Only let your conduct be worthy of the gospel of Christ, so that whether I come and see you or am absent, I may hear of your affairs, that you stand fast in one spirit, with one mind striving together for the faith of the gospel"* Philippians 1:27. Now, with that being said, it is only wise to get out of your own way to embrace the *Tree of Life*, take a risk, or play the Game of Life.

I am constantly asked, "Is gambling a sin?" Let's set the record straight regarding this big hypocritical behavior called gambling. First and foremost, gambling is NOT a sin. If one would say that it is—then they must also say that taking a risk is a sin as well. Let me explain, how often do we gamble with our lives? How often do we take a risk? How often do we lay our lives on the line to save another life? How often do we play the stock market? How often do we make a bet? Are we gambling with our lives every time we pick up a new sex partner, are we gambling with our lives when our partner cheats on us, or are we gambling with our lives when we find a date on the internet? Or, better yet, when we live from paycheck to paycheck, are we not taking a gamble with our lives and the lives of our family? Every time that we take our family on vacation, knowing that we still have bills to pay, is that not a gamble? Are these not all a form of gambling? We look down on one person for gambling in a casino or playing the lotto, but how often do we gamble, not even realizing that we are gambling? It would be fair to say that gambling is not a sin; however, anything that we abuse, misuse, or sell our souls for, feeds our sinful nature causing the urge to become bigger, stronger, and consuming, mentally, physically, emotionally, and spiritually that leads to the ultimate SIN, whatever that may be. These are some questions that we must ask ourselves when it comes down to whether or not we are over-indulging, acting carelessly, acting out of foolishness, or acting on faith. There is a thin line between doing what's right or acting out of our sinful nature; however, I am going to make it real simple for one to understand if their nature of gambling or taking a risk, is or is not sinful. From my perspective, it is indeed the intent of the HEART that determines our sin! If we understand the "Why" of what we are doing—we can determine whether it lines up with Godly character or not.

In order to have what we want in life, we must take some sort of risk. I've always heard "Nothing risked, nothing gained!" It has been proven to be a true statement, time and time again.   It has not changed, and it will NEVER change......for it is the LAW OF THE LAND. Just think about every time that we eat a meal someone took a risk or someone gambled with their crops or livestock to put food on our table. This is not a Bible study lesson; this is indeed "A Life Lesson" that we must understand before we turn up our nose at someone who's indulging in the area of their life that we do not indulge in. If the truth is told, we all have this ONE PLACE in our lives that we gamble with; therefore, we must remember that we have all sinned and fallen short. Today, reflect on the things, the people, or the places that you are gambling with and make sure that it is indeed a positive Gamble and not a negative one. Lastly, let me leave you with a little testimony, I am a massive risk-taker—I started writing with my mistakes and all. I did not care who saw or judged them—I was on a mission. I was talked about, criticized, and laughed at because of my mistakes; but, I did not stop because they could not hear the VOICE that I heard from within. As a matter of fact, I would not be where I am today, spewing out Divine Wisdom as such, if I would have listened to the ridicules of those who were not gifted in the area that I am anointed in. Now, the once naysayers are gleaning from the same wisdom that they made fun of…..you can call it a gamble or a risk—I count it all the same because my HEART is in the right place. After all of the rejection, torment, atrocities, hatefulness, and people taking my kindness for a weakness—I lived by my infamous quote that I have not deviated from, "Life is a Game, You Play or Be Played, and If You Play by God's Rules, You Will Win Every Time, Guaranteed!" If you live by that principle, while guarding your tongue, keeping your emotions in check, not allowing people to plant a mind-germ in your head to negatively control you, and pray for God's will to be done in your life—there's no limit to what you can achieve. You have my word on that!

CHAPTER 4

Accountability At Its Best

Do you feel blocked with nowhere to turn? Does your life feel like a trap waiting to snap you up at any given moment? Do you feel as if the whole world is against you? My friend, let me tell you, "Join the crowd!" Everyone has these feelings from time to time, especially around the New Year or a Birthday, everyone wants to change something. In my opinion, we do not have to wait for the New Year or a Birthday to start over, set a goal, play our role, or make changes—we are in the here and now. Our change starts with a decision, a decision to get out of our own way.

Make no mistake about it, the things around us may not change, our circumstances may not change, and we cannot trade-in our family members for new ones; therefore, there are certain people, places, and things that we must deal with until our change comes without making excuses. With a made-up mind, it is imperative to play our hand close to our chest with a new, positive, productive, and fruitful mindset—then rest assured, change for the better is inevitable. Simply keep in mind that there is a time and a season for everything under the sun; therefore, when our season arrives, no one can stop it, but we must be ready, willing, and able to embrace it with the appropriate attitudinal mindset.

I have found that the best way to get out of our own way is to do a character check-up. I must admit that it is hard to see ourselves through our own eyes; therefore, we must begin to understand some of the signals that others are subconsciously giving us. The most obvious signal that we need a character check-up is when people around us are trying not to become like us and/or avoid us at all cost. This tell-tell sign reveals that our overbearing creed has overshadowed our desire to exhibit Godly character in our lives, as well as into the lives of others. In so many words, when we are busy trying to correct the lives of others, and they see that our lives are in disarray, they will instinctively pull away; therefore, blocking our effectiveness.

Incidentally, please do not get a character check-up confused with envy or jealousy—envy or jealousy will cause the person who wants to be like us, to avoid us at all cost as well. Therefore, we need to set an example, and the very things that we do not like others to do to us, do not do it to them. Moreover, when it comes down to having and maintaining a positive mental attitude, jealousy or envy has a way of creeping in to steal friendships, marriages, partnerships, etc. It is jealousy or envy that causes someone to try to hold us back, oppress us, sabotage our success, speak ill-will against us, create chaos, and the list goes on. On the other hand, exercising wisdom from the *Book of Proverbs* will enable us to become intellectual, astute in our ways, keen in our way of thinking, formulative in our way of planning, articulative in our way of expression, discerning in our ways of operation, instinctual in the nudges from within, and teachable.

Our best bet is to focus on *"being wise as serpents and innocent as doves."* Matthew 10:16, while succeeding in all that we do to produce good fruit. Most of us do not want to agree with where our fruits are falling; better yet, we dare not assume responsibility for anything that puts our image at stake. For the most part, it doesn't matter whether we want to paint a picture-perfect life or not if we do not understand the type of fruit that's falling in and around our life, it is impossible to make the appropriate corrections. In my opinion, the positive or negative fruits that we bear will always fall close by; however, when the positive fruit falls, simply allow the fruit to remain to ensure that it bears much fruit. Now, for the negative fruit, we must quickly pick up the fallen fruit, turn it into a positive and replant it into fertile ground. This is one of the best ways that I have found to keep negative traits from bearing fruit in our future. The purpose of **"Secret Wisdom"** is to give everyone the opportunity to look around to see the results of his or her fallen fruits. If our fallen fruits are negative, we are now equipped with the information on how to make the necessary corrections. By doing so, it ensures that our life doesn't become a direct reflection of what we DO NOT want.

Anyone can proclaim to have good character, anyone can pretend to have good character, and anyone can play the role of having good character; however, good character starts from within, working itself outwardly. Yes, from within the depths of our very own soul the contents of our heart will be revealed in our actions, reactions, thoughts, and the lack thereof. When it comes down to attitude, we must take our character into consideration because they come as a package deal—it is highly impossible to change our attitude without evaluating our character, and we can't change our character without evaluating our attitude. It is through the oneness of the two that gives birth to our behavioral pattern that may or may not be conducive to the expectations that we may have set for ourselves. That is why some people make promises of changing their ways, but cannot understand why they keep falling short of doing so; therefore, we learn how to pretend or create a different face for the situation, circumstance, or the person that we are dealing with. Now, the question we are dealing with here is, "Can a Leopard change his or her spots?" As we know in all honesty, the answer is NO. We are who we are; however, we can positively change our thoughts, perception, or attitude about our spots, which creates a workable awareness invoking self-control. Once we are able to control self, our positive spots will begin to outshine the negative ones, if we focus on doing what's right oppose to doing wrong. And, regardless of what others say or think about us, it's what we say or think that really matters. Simply focus on doing good deeds by positively encouraging, building, and helping others; and, watch how they will begin to see beyond our spots or characteristic flaws, as our good begins to outweigh the bad.

Your attitude, character traits, thoughts, and actions will be the determining factor in whether you build, destroy, or pick up debris. However, if you want lasting success, *"Do not forsake wisdom, and she will guard you; love her, and she will watch over you. The beginning of wisdom is to acquire wisdom, and with all your acquiring, get an understanding. Prize wisdom and she will exalt you;*

Chapter 4 | Ruby Fleurcius

she will honor you if you embrace her." Proverbs 4:6-8. If you can reach beyond your self-imposed limitations to embrace wisdom wholeheartedly, [She] Wisdom will help you to get out of your own way, so that you can begin to "Own IT" as *"your gift will begin to make room for you setting you before men in high places."* Proverbs 18:16.

How do we deal with constantly being judged? The factor of judgment is all around us, and we will never get away from it physically. It is indeed the physical aspects of an individual that gives others a bird's-eye view of what's taking place from within, mentally, emotionally, and spiritually. In my opinion, we become a victim of judgment when we do not understand that we have a FREE-WILL or misuse our FREE-WILL to victimize others. Judgment is designed to encourage, motivate, or empower us toward righteousness; it is not designed to discourage, disable, humiliate, or betray others out of selfishness, envy, or hatred. When we become truly accountable for our actions, reactions, and the lack thereof, we are better able to overcome our fears, we are better able to deal with rejection, we are better able to deal with the lack of recognition, we are better able to discipline ourselves, and we are better able to take responsibility for our lives without having to shift the blame to make ourselves appear as if we are more than what we are. As a matter of fact, we are who we are for a reason, and if we are doing the right thing, then there is no reason to waste our mental energy on those who are not conducive to our well-being or those who are trying to place us in bondage mentally, emotionally, physically, spiritually, or financially. Therefore, it is always best to steer away from those who judge your condition; while drawing close to those who invest in your potential. Your strength lies in your ability to choose a circle of empowerment, not a circle of defeat!

The best way to esteem self is to think positive—when we look for the good in all things, it will naturally release chemicals within our brain that will boost how we think of ourselves. For example, when we exercise, our bodies release hormones to help balance our ability to think, react, and overcome; without it, we become stressed out, depressed, and disease stricken. And, if we have a desire to boost our esteem, all we have to do is change the way we think positively, become quick to forgive, enjoy life, and exercise our bodies. In my opinion, this cannot be accomplished with a pill, alcohol, drugs, or another person; it must come from within. When we become a "TEAM" with ourselves mentally, emotionally, spiritually, and physically, our "ESTEEM" will bow down to us. Listen, the word "ESTEEM" tells us what we need to do, but it is often overlooked because we are conditioned **NOT** to see it.........ES TEEM or IS TEAM? Yes, what we need to do to build our self-esteem is hidden in plain sight. When we team up with ourselves, there is no limit on what we can achieve. From now on out, give yourself a boost of your positive self, it will do wonders for you and the people around you. Trust me, you are your best cheerleader; therefore, you cannot go wrong with a positive mindset— your ESTEEM depends on it.

CHAPTER 5

The Power of Vujá Dé

Are we really able to change the way we think about a negative situation? Absolutely. I am living proof of it—I never knew that this type of WISDOM would flow out of my lions until I changed my perspective and trained my mind to obey me! Listen, we have power over our mind, as well as our thinking process—we just have to TRAIN our mind to obey us. Today, it is my reasonable service to share my perspective on WISDOM. When God created heaven and earth, He envisioned what He wanted, and it became so. We are created in His image, so what makes us any different? We have more power than we give ourselves credit for. As a matter of fact, not only do we need to have a vision of what we desire, we also need to believe in that Vision as well. In Exodus Chapter 3, at the burning bush, God gave Moses the vision of delivering the Children of Israel out of Egypt, and He also gave him instructions on how to do so. God knew that the Children of Israel lacked vision, so He gave Moses specific instructions on what to say to ignite the hope of those that were struggling with their faith. As the Children of Israel struggled, they still prayed, and even though they prayed out of habit—they still had some form of hope! Regardless of whether or not their vision was lining up with what they were praying for, their vision became enslaved by the limitation of their environment. It is amazing how that cycle has continued throughout—we are still battling with that same form of vision enslavement today.

I have learned throughout the years to envision what you want to become a reality, and it will be so. Therefore, in order to prevent the cycle of "Déjà vu" in your life, where history keeps repeating itself, you need to create something a little different. When in doubt about your vision, or if you are not sure about something in your life, start writing it out like a **Breadcrumb Trail** to free your mind, getting your thoughts on paper. This is done by asking yourself fact-finding questions. By doing so, you will create what I call **VUJÁ DÉ**, which is the opposite of déjà vu. This is where you are able to see your life from a different perspective. When you are able to shift the perspective on your life, you are then able to shift your vision; therefore, creating a more desirable result rather than having history to repeat itself constantly, wasting precious time. If you do not shift your perspective, your life will continue the same cycle, with different scenes, characters, etc.; because if the same thing keeps happening, there is a lesson that you are not learning, and you are REQUIRED to shift your perspective to get a different result. Trust me; it's not them, it's not "IT"—it is YOU! Your WISDOM is waiting for you to make a decision!

Is your cup half-full, or is your cup half-empty? I have been asked this question time without number, and my answer has always remained the same. I am not settling for my cup to be half-full or half-empty when I am indeed the cup. I take ownership, so it doesn't matter whether my cup is half-full, half empty, completely full, or completely empty, "I am IT!" We are conditioned to always say that our cup is half-full, so why can we not be conditioned to take ownership of our lives? Passing the buck just to be accepted or to eliminate the feeling of rejection is unacceptable. The *Fifth Secret of Proverbs* is that we must learn how to OWN IT, whatever our "IT" is, regardless if it's right, wrong, or indifferent. [She]Wisdom requires responsibility to that in which has our attention. And, what I have found is that owning it helps us to get an understanding, and denying it inhibits our ability to become true to ourselves. For this reason, Proverbs 3:5-6 advocates getting an understanding by saying, *"Trust in the Lord with all your heart, and lean not on your own understanding; in all your ways acknowledge Him, and He shall direct your paths."*

Now, let me ask a question, "In Genesis *22: 1-18,* would it have been acceptable if Abraham would have repeated to others that God had told him to sacrifice his only son?" The answer is NO! It would have been utter chaos—Abraham would have suffered the severe repercussions of being rejected by others. That's why we have to keep certain things to ourselves, "OWN IT" and allow God to work it out. The opinions of others can and will detour us if we are caught in a web of self-denial, self-deception, insecurity, or lack of direction.

When it comes down to taking ownership, or responsibility for our actions, reactions, or the lack thereof, rejection is grandfathered in automatically to test the waters, so to speak. And, for that reason, there are some things in life that we cannot just tell anybody. As a matter of fact, there are some places in life that we can only allow God to go with us. When we are in a fragile state of being, and we cannot handle any more rejection, it is better to avoid it at all cost. I am not saying ignore the cause of the rejection, or harden our heart to rejection; I am saying that we must do our best to avoid taking ourselves mentally or emotionally where we do not desire to be, in order to protect our sanity. For our sake, if this requires us to keep things to ourselves while taking it to God in prayer, then that's what needs to be done. However, in the midst of prayer, we must not forget to get an understanding of why we feel the way we feel while allowing God to heal whatever is going on within the depths of our soul.

Rejection is born out of fear, anger, jealousy, envy, lack of love, or conditioning—we will find that the rejected, rejects others to cover up their wounds of insecurity. Please understand that we are all insecure about something; however, an extremely insecure person can be spotted by their jealousy/envy of others, their extreme ability to brow-beat others, their ability to criticize others about the same things that they are guilty of, their ability to profusely gossip about others, their ability to use the past against others as leverage to get what they want, their ability to be insensitive to the feelings/emotions of others, and their ability to abuse others mentally, physically, emotionally, or spiritually without giving it a second thought. Unresolved or ignored insecurity causes one to look for weaknesses in others to actually hide or cover up their very own hidden weaknesses or the lack of love.

There are times when we feel that love has eluded us; but the truth is, true love resides within us. In my opinion, like attracts like, and if we do not truly love ourselves unselfishly, we will find that we unknowingly drive away the people who are making an attempt to extend his or her love toward us. It is not that love doesn't exist; it is a matter of whether we reject or embrace the love that's coming our way. If we are not sure how to love, then we need to learn—it's okay to pick up a book or take a class on love. If we have never experienced love, then we need to find it within ourselves first, by making a list of the good/bad things, positive/negative things, or the right/wrong things about ourselves, as well as the fears that we have that prevents us from loving ourselves and others. If we want to attract more love our way, we must be willing to give it; but, in order to give it, we must possess it—we cannot drink from a well that's dried up. The *Book of Proverbs* says, *"Honour the LORD with thy substance, and with the firstfruits of all thine increase: So shall thy barns be filled with plenty, and thy presses shall burst out with new wine."* Proverbs 3:9-10. Most would associate this proverbial scripture with money; but [She]Wisdom says that this scripture applies to anything that we have a desire to bear fruit, positively or negatively. The Law of Reciprocity is in effect with or without our permission; therefore, we must become ever so cognizant about what we give, accept, and reject. To have more of that in which we desire, we must forget about the hurts, pains, and reservations that we may have about giving, receiving, and rejecting love while embracing the truth about our reality.

The truth about a circumstance, event, situation, or even about us could very well be a hard pill to swallow, especially when it cuts really, really deep. Whenever the truth hurts, it's very important that we understand the reasons why. It is imperative that we resolve or control the emotions that are attached to the hurt. Otherwise, we will fall victim to our own untruths about ourselves, our situation, our circumstance, or event. However, if we trust ourselves enough to live a lie, eventually the truth will surface, because it is harder to remember lies that are told in and out of sequence; therefore, making rejection an inevitable consequence of the trust that's broken. In my opinion, lying to buy time is a big time waster, when the truth will yield much better results, or when we can simply plead the 5th. We can't go wrong trusting ourselves with the truth about who we are, even if we are rejected.

I would say rejection is not such a bad thing to become exposed to—once an individual can accept rejection, he or she will become able to overcome obstacles that others would back away from. According to statistics, 80% of success is obtained by 20% of the population, so there are a lot of people who are left behind because rejection has booted them out of that 20% of dreamers and doers. In so many words, 20% of people are willing to do what the other 80% are unwilling or conditioned not to do. Of course, some may not believe in the 80/20 rule, but if rejection is a weakness, it is now time to overcome it to ensure that the fear of failure will not prevent the heart's desire from becoming a reality. Furthermore, from this point forward, if someone rejects us or what we have to offer, simply say "Thank you" and move on. My secret to the 80/20 rule is that we will be rejected by 80% of the people that are not designed to fit into our lives; and, if we do not allow rejection to break us, it then prepares us for the 20% of the positive people, places, and things that will help us to soar into the 80% success category, even with our issues as long as we are not lying to ourselves about our reality. Just remember a positive attitude does cause rules to become amended for our sake if we believe. So, I would say that a positive attitude does account for something; especially, when people are secretly rejecting us because they don't feel good about themselves.

Now, having a positive attitude does not mean that we will not have a negative thought, nor does it mean that we will always do or say the right thing—what it means is that we will positively take responsibility for our actions, reactions, thoughts or the lack thereof. Shifting the blame for what we do, say, or become does not exhibit responsibility, nor does it help us resolve our issues or character flaws. In my opinion, the sooner we own up to what we do, say, or become, the sooner we can make the positive adjustments in what has caused us to focus on the negative more than the positive aspects of our lives. Of course, we are all sensitive in some way—some more sensitive than others; however, the key is to learn how to deal with our sensitivities. Most often, our sensitivities are usually the result of some sort of pain or trauma, but it only becomes a problem when we allow it to get out of control, or we play the role of being a victim. Playing the victim will get us attention, it will get us what feels like love, or it will get us sympathy; but, it does not bring us wholeness. In my opinion, playing the victim will keep us looking for the next emotional quick-fix that feeds our internal conflict; as a matter of fact, playing the victim role will only allow us enough room to play ourselves in the end, if we do not positively change our mentality about the situation, circumstance, or event.

If victimization has caused us to feel lonely, depressed, abandoned, and/or helpless, please seek help—find someone that is trustworthy and talk to them. Now, with that being said, the ultimate goal is to live our lives in victory, while becoming a mentor for the real victims of unfortunate circumstances. Today, start looking for the good in everyone and watch how the natural goodness begins to rise up out of you. Just remember that you were born to love and be loved! So what, if you have been hurt—don't let it take what truly belongs to you, and that is your right to be happy. Be true to yourself, love like you have never been hurt before, and watch how you begin to heal beyond all human understanding—as your well begins to overflow, quenching the thirst of the longing that you have from within to better prepare you for spiritual warfare.

CHAPTER 6

Spiritual Warfare

Is spiritual warfare real? Absolutely! Spiritual warfare is all around us, and it has been since Adam and Eve—it has been battling for its territory, and it's not going anywhere. In my opinion, spiritual warfare is real, and it can become very dangerous if we are not prepared for it or uninformed about it. Most often, we have been conditioned to think that spiritual warfare is not real or that it simply does not exist, but if we look around to see what is taking place right now, we will understand that this is not about us, it is a spiritual battle that's bigger than us. According to Ephesians 6:12, *"For we wrestle not against flesh and blood, but against principalities, against powers, against the rulers of the darkness of this world, against spiritual wickedness in high places."* It is a battle that's destroying families, it's a battle that's destroying faith, it's a battle that's destroying hope, and it's a battle that's destroying our ability to trust in those who are designed to serve and protect. This type of mental or emotional enslavement should not exist, but it does! We are living in fear in the land of the FREE! We are allowing it into our homes, churches, workplaces, communities, etc. Although, some of this MIND CONTROL GERM phenomenon is being forced upon us; however, we must become mentally, emotionally, physically, and spiritually strong to endure this type of warfare. This is a STRONGHOLD that has us bound right now, we must recognize it for what it is—until then, we are going to become a laughing stock for all onlookers to see that we are not so free after all if we are bound mentally. We are not just fighting for the peace in our homes, we are fighting for our loved ones, we are fighting for the peace of our nation, and we are fighting for the Kingdom of God. Once we recognize this battle for what it is, we are better able to become equipped for it—as I said previously, violence is not the answer—PRAYER is. Remember, this is a God ruled nation, and if we are trusting man to fix this issue, our trust is indeed in the wrong place. The Book of Proverbs in the Bible tells us more about Godly character that will keep our families and our Nation together, but it is overlooked, then we wonder why social media has taken over. It is always best to pray over your loved ones before they leave home, pray for them when they get back, pray for them before they go to sleep at night, keep yourself prayed up, and pray for everyone. God's grace and mercy are real, He is no respecter of persons, He reigns on the just and the unjust alike; and, He loves us all no matter what! Fast and pray for the Land of the FREE, your mental, physical, emotional, and spiritual freedom depends on it!

The *Book of Proverbs* is full of instructions and has a very low tolerance regarding our behavior. [She] Wisdom does not hold back regarding the correction that is required to embrace her, she says in Proverbs 15:32 *"If we reject discipline, we only harm ourselves; but if we listen to correction, we grow in understanding."* And, she also says in Proverbs 1:30-33 that *"Because they rejected my advice and turned down my correction, they will surely get what's coming to them: they'll be forced to eat the fruit of their wicked ways; they'll gorge themselves on the consequences of their choices. You see, it's turning away from me that brings death to the simple, and it's self-satisfaction that destroys the fools. But whoever listens to me will dwell safely, and will be secure, without fear of evil."*

One would never openly call themselves a hypocrite, but our actions would definitely speak of such behavior. However, in the *Book of Proverbs*, that type of behavior is often referred to as folly, or the behavior of a fool. Although I personally will not call anyone a fool, I am only making reference to the foolish behavior that would cause one to get a checkup from the neck up. As one would have it, our episodes of folly would become buried away or stored as a skeleton in one's closet; however, it is imperative that our behavior becomes replaced with wisdom to safeguard our future. [She] Wisdom says that our future begins with this number one rule: *"Let your foot rarely be in your neighbor's house, lest he become weary of you and hate you."* Proverbs 25:16-17. When we are in and out of the houses of others, it's hard to take care of our own house; therefore, leaving our own house unkept. [She] Wisdom is adamant about us following this rule to prevent unnecessary chaos and confusion from running wild exposing our skeletons.

What do we do with the skeletons that are trying to come out of the closet? I would say, "BURY THEM." Make no mistake about it, we all have skeletons; and when we keep our skeletons in the closet, it is a possibility that when our emotions run high, we may go to the closet to expose that in which should be put behind us. When we become comfortable reliving our past, it becomes hard to embrace the newness of life; therefore, causing us to attract the people, places and things that cater to the needs, wants, and desires of what's in our closet. The Bible clearly states, *"When I was a child, I spoke as a child; but when I became an adult, I put away childish things."* However, when peer pressure kicks in, that is a whole new ball game; and, here is what Proverbs 2:12-19 says that it wants to do for you, *"To deliver you from the way of evil, from the man who speaks perverse things; from those who leave the paths of uprightness, To walk in the way of darkness; who delight in doing evil, And rejoice in the perversity of evil; whose paths are crooked, And who are devious in their ways; to deliver you from the strange woman, From the adulteress who flatters with her words; that leaves the companion of her youth, And forgets the covenant of her God; for her house sinks down to death, And her tracks lead to the dead; none who go to her return again, Nor do they reach the paths of life."*

[She] Wisdom is a stickler regarding our hypocritical behavior, especially when we judge others for the same things that we are guilty of. The moment that we become big headed or arrogant about being perfect, [She] Wisdom will give us a mental flashback as a warning to correct our behavior. If it is not corrected [She] Wisdom will knock a few notches off our belt; and if still left uncorrected, she will bring us down to reality exposing all of our skeletons. Please do not allow your skeletons, your weaknesses, or hang-ups to cause you to fall by the wayside because of a deaf ear to wisdom.

If people are chirping in your ear about wrong doings, walk away. If people are pressuring you to violate your conscience, walk away. If people are pressuring you for your secrets, walk away; as long as you know and understand the truth about you does not mean that you have to tell the whole world unless it's positive. If it's negative or condemning, put it away; and if you cannot bury it, then keep your innermost secrets or your most incriminating skeletons to yourself. You really don't know who is or who is not envious of who you are, what you do, or what you may become; and, if they feel threatened in any way, they may use your past against you as leverage. As a rule of thumb, play your cards close to your chest, because God has allowed certain things to happen to you for your growth and not your demise; and I must say that it's hard to embrace the *Tree of life* when you are allowing the skeletons of your past to create a thicket of your old mindset. Let it go and move on.

To truly embrace the Power of our Attitude, we must understand that no one is absolutely perfect, we are born into a World of Sin, and we are all subject to human nature. If we look around us, we will see that we will never have to train a child to do wrong—they will naturally do the wrong thing for *"Foolishness is bound up in the heart of a child."* Proverbs 22:15; yet, it is our responsibility to teach them to do right! This same concept applies to our attitude—our mind will naturally gravitate to the negative until we train it to look automatically for the positive.

Why do we always want what we don't have? I must say that it is human nature—we are born with the desire for more. This could very well be a good thing, or it could very well be a bad thing, depending upon the intent of our heart. The intent of the heart will determine whether our desire for more is just or unjust. Of course, we all have our likes and dislikes, but when we are not sure of them, we will tend to follow the likes and dislikes of others that feed into the discontentment of what we already have. Our freedom of choice is the one reason why we do what we do, say what we say, and want what we want; however, the key is to become a good steward over what we have first, and then set goals to attain more. For example, if we want a better job, we must exude the Spirit of Excellence in the job that we already have. If we want a better car, we must take care of the one we have. If we have a desire for a new relationship, we must make sure that we did not mistreat anyone in our previous relationship. If we want to lose weight, we must be happy with ourselves at our present weight while developing a healthy mental attitude. As the list goes on, we must master our present state of being before setting our minds on other things, because wanting people, places, and things for the wrong reason will do us a great disservice. Most of the time we will not miss what we have lost until it's gone; besides, most of our blessings are right under our nose, but we are too blind to see it because of our human nature. It is imperative that we make sure that we become a good steward over what we have to ensure that we want people, places and things for the right reason. By doing so, this will ensure that greed, discontentment, envy, or selfishness does not cause us to lose our integrity or devalue what we already have.

As your check-up becomes a way of life for you, let me make mention of the *Sixth Secret of Proverbs:* a Proverb a day, will indeed keep the Doctor away. When we allow Proverbs to become a source of our daily meditation, it secretly infuses you with a personal power that you did not know existed.

CHAPTER 7

The Truth About Us

The *Tree of Life* prides itself on integrity. When in doubt about anything, [She] Wisdom advises that integrity will take us where deception never will. And, with that in mind, the *Seventh Secret of Proverbs* is to exercise integrity at all cost, because righteousness will set a Spiritual Covering over our lives to protect, guide, and heal. [She] Wisdom says that integrity is our secret shield and buckler, without this covering, we leave ourselves open to folly, temptation, and waywardness.

Integrity is not about bossing people around, manipulating them, or bullying them. It is when we can exhibit strength and authority to do what's right without even saying a word, or without someone telling us to do so. [She] Wisdom says that *"Whoever walks in integrity walks securely, but whoever takes crooked paths will be found out."* Proverbs 10:9. Is integrity really worth using when our back is up against the wall? In my opinion, we should not wait until our back is up against the wall to use it, we should exercise integrity in all that we do, say, and become. And, being that this is [She] Wisdom's pet peeve, we must tread carefully because *"These six things doth the LORD hate: yea, seven are an abomination unto him: A proud look, a lying tongue, and hands that shed innocent blood, a heart that deviseth wicked imaginations, feet that be swift in running to mischief, a false witness that speaketh lies, and he that soweth discord among brethren."* Proverbs 6:16-19.

Mercy is indeed a prerequisite of integrity that [She] Wisdom will not budge an inch on; and, she will take us down quickly if we pass judgment on the very thing that we are guilty of. *"He who oppresses the poor reproaches his Maker, but he who honors Him has mercy on the needy."* Proverbs 14:31. Not only that, when we take it upon ourselves to kick someone when they are down, oppose to helping them if it's within our scope of doing so—[She] Wisdom will bring that very thing that we lacked mercy regarding back to our own home! Therefore, *"If thine enemy be hungry, give him bread to eat; and if he be thirsty, give him water to drink: For thou shalt heap coals of fire upon his head, and the LORD shall reward thee."* Proverbs 25:21-22. From this point forward, there is no need to worry about what people are doing; we must worry about what we are doing, saying, and becoming to ensure that are blessings remain and that we keep our hands blessed at all times. We never want to curse our own hands because we cannot control our emotions. Thus it is better to put our emotions aside and exercise integrity at all cost; for *"The fear of man brings a snare, but whoever trusts in the Lord shall be safe."* Proverbs 29:25

In today's time, with the fast movement of social media, we can become known for what we want to be known for;

however, once our integrity is lost through telling lies, it is hard to regain. *"Lying lips are an abomination to the Lord, but those who deal truthfully are His delight."* Proverbs 12:22. We have learned in a previous chapter that a good name is chosen; and, what we do not realize is that our integrity, credibility, and character are a part of who we are. Who cares about a name, integrity, or credibility as long as we are getting what we want, right? Wrong, whether we are at the top or the bottom of the ladder of success, we need to exercise caution when our integrity is involved, because we may not be able to undo something once it is done.

Proverbs 20:7 says, *"The righteous man walks in his integrity; his children are blessed after him."* Our children are indeed riding on the integrity that we exercise today; therefore, we must exercise extreme caution when doing or saying something that has the potential to come back to bite us in the butt. For Proverbs 11:3 tells us that *"The integrity of the upright will guide them, but the crookedness of the treacherous will destroy them."* Of course, we will always appear right in our own eyes, we will not be able to please everyone 100% of the time, we will not be right 100% of the time, nor will we be wrong 100% of the time; but, we can exercise our integrity 100% of the time. Just remember, integrity is a choice, and every time we use it, it grows stronger, especially when coupled with forgiveness. However, if we have trust issues, then that's a whole new ball game.

[She] Wisdom reveals that we are all born into a trust matrix with supernatural trust. In the infant stages of life, we are designed to trust life, our parents, etc.; basically, we trust everything whether it's good or bad, right or wrong. When we step outside of our matrix of trust, we will find that we will begin to lower our standards, allowing negative debris into our lives. And, once our lives become contaminated, our trust will become seriously mangled by our superficial addictions, vices, infidelities, and abuses that compromise our integrity. I have found that in order to mastermind our integrity, we must understand and exercise the power of forgiveness. As a matter of fact, without forgiveness, it is impossible to keep and maintain our integrity. In so many words, grudges will keep our integrity chained to the negative emotions of the past that will constantly invoke the spirit of jealousy, envy, and/or confusion when we least expect it. To eliminate or soothe a hurt, we must find and admit to the cause/reason of the hurt, as well as the role that we have played. Please understand that there are always three sides to every story: our side, their side, and the TRUTH; and, if we allow others to validate our hurt or take sides in our hurt, we will begin to feed known or unknown weaknesses that may prevent us from discovering or understanding the truth behind the hurt. Of course, it's only natural to want others to justify our negative feelings, but that will only push us further into a rebellious state of being. For [She] Wisdom says, *"Do not be envious of evil men, nor desire to be with them; for their minds devise violence, and their lips talk of trouble."* Proverbs 24:1-2.

Once we begin to rebel against life, we will find that life will begin to expose the people, places and things that contribute to our condition. Once we know what pushes our button or violates our integrity, we must stay away from it; and, if we are not able to stay away, limit contact or exposure to it. My philosophy is to keep it simple and stop allowing people to chat in our ears before we have a talk with God about whatever it is. If we find ourselves hurt about something or someone, when speaking with God, we must evaluate the three sides of the story: our side, their side, and the truth. [She] Wisdom says, by doing so, it allows us to understand our role in the situation, circumstance, or event, it allows us to forgive, it allows us to take our power back, and it allows us to move on as if we have never been hurt before. As a result, [She] Wisdom guarantees that this will keep integrity on our side while keeping the silent enemy from within at peace.

Today, reclaim your integrity—it is your life-line to your peace, prosperity, and sanity. Once that is accomplished, from this point forward, *"Do not withhold good from those to whom it is due, when it is in the power of your hands to do so."* Proverbs 3:27. If you can help someone, help them. If you can encourage someone, encourage them. If you can love someone, love them. If you can motivate someone, do it. If you can bless someone, bless them with no strings attached. I firmly believe that if for some reason you can't see your way through something, give your way through it—trust me, paying it forward really works. I am living proof. And, this is where [She] Wisdom taught me the *Eighth Secret of Proverbs:* Filling the needs of others can and will open the door to getting our own personal needs, wants, or desires met. She [wisdom] advises that when we open our hands first, that enables God to open His hands: As Scripture concurs, *"Give, and it will be given to you: good measure, pressed down, shaken together, and running over will be put into your bosom. For with the same measure that you use, it will be measured back to you."* Luke 6:38.

How do we get rid of emotional, physical, mental, or spiritual pains? The first step to getting rid of any form of pain is to acknowledge it. Denial is only a temporary sedative to sugar coat our ability to lie to ourselves. As we begin to understand and digest the outcome of our election, we must realize that the people's choice may or may not be God's choice. This reminds me of the Biblical story of King Saul, Israel's First King. This is a story where the people wanted a king, and God granted them what they wanted. There are times when God will allow us to have what we desire in order to teach us a valuable lesson regarding our inner bred prejudices. In my opinion, this moment in time has revealed a lot of unresolved prejudices that are hidden in the depth of our soul. Better yet, the truth is that "Behind Closed Doors" we are all bias in some way, shape, or form—we are simply in denial of it; but, we are quick to look down on those who are honest about the way they feel. Division is among us right now—if we do not resolve the hidden biases of our past pains, we are headed for destruction mentally, physically, emotionally, and spiritually.

Our past, our present, and our future are in the palm of our hands; therefore, do not be quick to make a permanent decision regarding something or someone that's only designed to be temporary. If we dare to open our eyes to see, we will find that our blessings are hidden in plain sight, which are designed to bring us together and not divide us. When we love our neighbor as thyself, we will find that we can all live in peace regardless of who is in charge, regardless of our creed, and regardless of our deed. Today, I want you to always remember that this is indeed a God-Ruled Nation; and, you have to do your part in making this world a better place through the process of building up people opposed to bringing them down. Lastly, always remember to trust in God with all your heart and lean not to your own understanding because the Fight is Already Fixed, especially if you know what moves you.

CHAPTER 8

What Moves Us?

Is it possible that Abraham was secretly angry with God? It is definitely possible, because what man in his right mind would want to give up his child with a smile on his face. Although a slight bit of anger may have lain below the surface, Abraham was able to monitor it accordingly to achieve the desired outcome. He was able to take self out of the picture and place his faith in God, which resulted in him becoming a great and blessed nation. [She] Wisdom explains that *"Whoever has no rule over his own spirit is like a city broken down, without walls."* Proverbs 25:28; and that it's through our brokenness that we blame others to shift our responsibility.

Let me begin by saying; we cannot blame anyone for our emotions, especially anger. [She] Wisdom expresses that *"A fool shows his annoyance at once, but a prudent man overlooks an insult."* Proverbs 12:16. Anger is indeed an emotion that we will all have our share of, and it will always have its pros and cons. There are times when anger drives us to achieve more, there are times when anger will cause us to retreat, there are times when anger will cause us to open our eyes to reality, there are times when anger causes us to do unwise things that we end up regretting later, and there are times it will cause us to blow things out of proportion. Now, the one thing that anger will not do is override our will; therefore, we will always have the right to choose whether or not we will allow our anger to work for us or against us. When we allow anger to control our actions and reactions, that means that we agree with the results, positively or negatively. As the Book of Proverbs would have it, [She] Wisdom says, *"A fool always loses his temper, but a wise man holds it back."* Proverbs 29:11. *"A wise man fears the Lord and shuns evil, but a fool is hotheaded and reckless."* Proverbs 14:16. We do not have time to allow anger to cause us to wallow in the mud with its cousins called resentment, unforgiveness, or depression—we are in control, so we must manage anger wisely because the words that we choose when speaking are a reflection of who we are. For it is written, *"A soft answer turneth away wrath: but grievous words stir up anger. The tongue of the wise useth knowledge aright: but the mouth of fools poureth out foolishness."* Proverbs 15:1-2. Therefore, *"He who walks with wise men will be wise, but the companion of fools will suffer harm."* Proverbs 13:20. *"Do not associate with a man given to anger; or go with a hot-tempered man, lest you learn his ways, and find a snare for yourself."* Proverbs 22:24-25.

Often enough, we hear that our eyes are the window to our soul; however, we do not hear that what comes out of our mouth gives us a sneak peek at what we are thinking and feeling. If we desire to know where someone's head is at, simply listen to what's coming out of their mouth, especially when they are angry. Now, on the flip side of things, if we do not desire for someone to know where our head is at, it is better to keep our lips zipped, regardless of whether we are angry or not. When we become a good steward over what comes out of our mouth, and think about what we are saying before we say it—self-control then gives us an opportunity to safeguard the contents of our heart. Therefore, granting us the ability to think on our feet without being swayed by the negative opinions or actions of others in the midst of confusion.

What do you do when confusion breaks out? Stay calm! [She] Wisdom says that *"A man of knowledge uses words with restraint, and a man of understanding is even-tempered."* Proverbs 17:27. I know that it is easier said than done; however, if we do not feed confusion, more than likely it will calm down. If we feed confusion, it will grow, and the hunger for confusion will become stronger over a period of time. As a matter of fact, reacting to confusion will reveal certain weaknesses that should be left in the closet—so, choosing what, when, where, how, and why we react, is imperative in developing self-control to counteract it with something positive.

When dealing with a weakness, we will find that when exhibiting self-control in that particular area, temptation has a way of presenting itself quite often. As a matter of fact, if we look a little closer to our patterns or habits, we will find that stress has been the main trigger to our loss of control. For that reason, we must find peace from within quickly before our not so disciplined areas of our lives become exposed to the negative predators that are looking for our weakest link, or those who are looking to air our dirty laundry.

In my own personal experiences with controlling my anger, I felt as if God was making me weak, until [She]

Wisdom revealed to me, *"It is to a man's honor to avoid strife, but every fool is quick to quarrel." Proverbs 20:3. And, "Do not say, "I'll pay you back for this wrong!" Wait for the LORD, and he will deliver you."* Proverbs 20:22. After that, I no longer felt as if I was a little weakling; I realized that my strength was wrapped up in my self-control. Which brings me to the Ninth Secret of Proverbs: Exercising self-control is the cornerstone to keeping our strength and honor while [She] Wisdom governs that in which proceeds out of the gate of our mouth; therefore, giving us an advance opportunity to think before we speak. When you respond with wisdom, it really puts your naysayers at bay.

How do we know what moves us? We are indeed moved by our likes, dislikes, and conditioning—when we lack the understanding of them or when we are in denial of them, it brings about confusion from within, that will soon play itself out in our daily lives. For example, if we know beyond a shadow of a doubt that we are a great person with integrity, then we have nothing to prove to anyone, nor do we need to convince, fight, or deceive anyone about what's embedded in the depths of our soul. Now, on the other hand, if we are indecisive, manipulative, lack faith, or just downright trifling, then that is when we have to pretend, convince, or fight to get people to buy into our superficial façade. If we know what does or does not move us, we are better able to prevent division from within, we are better able to prevent division among others, and we are better able to remain neutral when people, places, and things get out of hand. All we have to do is ask ourselves, "Who are we trying to convince?" Trust me, the truth will always set us FREE.

Today, do not allow people to get into your head negatively; keep your zone positive, productive, and fruitful, letting nothing or no one take you out of that zone. Simply "Do You" and "Keep It Moving".....the guard that you place over your mind will protect you, your family, and your livelihood. Today, it's okay to hold yourself to a higher standard by embracing the Tree of Life—just hold steadfast to the Book of Proverbs, along with its Proverbial Wisdom, and rest assured, [She] Wisdom will take you places where you never imagined.

CHAPTER 9

Overcoming Obstacles

Obstacles are designed to keep us consumed, blind, blocked, or divided. If we do not find a way to recognize the obstacle for what it is, while putting it in its proper perspective, it will consume us with the mind-blocking actions, reactions, or thoughts that are attached to it. We will find that obstacles do not come alone; they come with their cousins called depression, oppression, and anxiety that attaches and feeds on our negative emotions that will cause us to implode or explode with unexplainable mental and physical sicknesses or diseases.

How can we overcome depression, oppression, or anxiety? Acknowledgment is the first step to overcoming anything. If that is how we are feeling, acknowledge it, develop a plan not to feel that way, give it to God through the power of prayer. If we need to grieve then do so...it is necessary for the human psyche to move on mentally or emotionally after some form of loss, and then move on physically. Denial suppresses and deepens our state of depression, oppression, and anxiety; therefore, making us extra sensitive, controlling, manipulative, or emotionally overbearing. As a matter of fact, it will also keep us on an emotional rollercoaster ride depending on what's going on in our lives at the time. I have found that the quickest way to get out of a depressive, oppressive, or anxious state is to laugh—it is hard to be happy and sad at the same time.

I make it my business to have an equal balance of serious and fun moments in my life to break the monotony of pumping out wisdom or doing business all the time—with my family; I am just ME. I do not pretend to be more than who I am, I laugh, I have fun, I speak country, and I crack jokes—that's what they know, and that's what they expect from me until we have a situation that requires me to put on my spiritual or business hat. I still live a normal life like everyone else; do I get upset with my family members? Absolutely! Do I allow my emotions to cause me to treat them any differently? Absolutely NOT! I live by certain standards, and I treat everyone with love, respect, and outright integrity even if I do not agree with their behavior. However, when I do business, I operate in reverse order—I put my personal life on the backburner and handle my business; taking the emotions of my personal life out of the equation to only deal with the business emotions at hand to ensure that my personal and professional life do not overlap.

Now, in order to operate in that fashion, we must get an understanding of how our emotions work; our emotions must choose a positive or negative state by remaining neutral, by having a positive response, or by having a negative response. Our emotions will choose one of the three, or an interchangeable combination of the three emotions which produces what we often call roller-coaster emotions. However, we must know what we are feeling in order to deal with our emotions appropriately to control certain types of behaviors, reactions, actions, or certain disrespectful things from coming out of our mouth. We do not have to think about what's positive or what's negative; our conscience already knows right from wrong—when we are doing the right thing we know it and when we are doing the wrong thing we know it as well. We can't go wrong with clean hands and a pure heart.

If we are depressed, oppressed, or anxious due to our own actions, reactions, or behaviors, then we need to make it our business to right a wrong, forgive ourselves, give it to God, and move on. It is time for you to smile your way to the top by thinking positive thoughts, doing what you enjoy doing, counteracting the negative with a positive, and creating a win-win situation out of everything.

We often struggle through life because we rely on our own understanding. I must admit that I am definitely guilty of behaving as such, especially when I have my emotional moments. Although, I do regroup quickly; however, I am not exempt from trying to stand under, stand over, and stand through things from my own perspective. I have also heard people say to use common sense when trying to get an understanding, but I beg to differ. [She] Wisdom affirmed to me that commonsense is not so common if we lack the understanding of our commonness, because *"A fool takes no pleasure in understanding, but only in expressing his opinion."* Proverbs 18:2. When in doubt, or our commonness is taking us for a loop, [She] Wisdom says that we must begin to *"Trust in the Lord with all our heart, and do not lean on our own understanding."* Proverbs 3:5. For that reason, we must find a way to get out of our own way and truly trust God as Abraham did.

If we honestly evaluate the situation that Abraham faced when asked to sacrifice his child Isaac, based on our human emotional perspective, we would consider it a negative situation. When in all actuality, it was a positive situation that presented itself as a negative. Abraham's story is designed to open our eyes to reality—our blessings will never appear as a blessing. However, if we open ourselves up to get an understanding of God's will and His ways, blessings will flow in our lives, regardless of how it may appear.

If we take a look back over our lives, our true blessings came from the people, places, things, obstacles, or challenges that appeared negative. Good things happen to bad people, and bad things happen to good people. [She] Wisdom concurs that it's just life, and in the midst of living *"Does not wisdom call? Does not understanding raise her voice?"* Proverbs 8:1. [She] Wisdom pulls no punches when it comes down to understanding—she will call us out, embarrass us, correct us, and bless us all at the same time. How wonderful is the *Book of Proverbs*, if we only would hear, listen, and understand the sound of her voice which reveals the positive and negative consequences of our thoughts, actions, and decisions. But, in all of our getting, *"Do not correct a scoffer, lest he hate you; rebuke a wise man, and he will love you. Give instruction to a wise man, and he will be still wiser; teach a just man, and he will increase in learning."* Proverbs 9:8-9. As I dug a little deeper, I then found the *Tenth Secret of Proverbs:* [She] Wisdom is no respecter of persons, God's blessings rain on the just and unjust alike. As long as we get an understanding of how the *Book of Proverbs* works, embrace what it has to offer, and follow instructions, [She] Wisdom will give us what we need. Whether we feel just or unjust in our ways, I must admit that applied wisdom has a way of turning a willing negative, naive person into a person of great esteem through these few acts of obedience.

Most often, what I have found is that people really do not understand the difference between a positive and a negative person. I found on several occasions that when I disagreed with a person's opinion or philosophy, they would consider it negative—when in fact, I did not say a negative word at all. So, when I am presented with a situation as such, I simply ask the question, "What did I say negative?" Of course, like clockwork, they were not able to answer the question, because they lacked the understanding in what I was saying. Disagreeing with someone or something doesn't make a person negative, what makes a person negative is one who degrades, disrespects, belittles, mocks, or criticizes others without making them better, or without offering them a positive plan of action. Better yet, [She] Wisdom says, *"A worthless person, a wicked man, Is the one who walks with a false mouth, Who winks with his eyes, who signals with his feet, Who points with his fingers; Who with perversity in his heart devises evil continually, Who spreads strife."* Proverbs 6:12-14. Just remember, a positive person or a person with a positive mental attitude does not wallow or agree to the folly of others—they may ask fact-finding questions to help the individual, or they may prevent a negative individual from zapping all of their positive energy, but they will *"Keep their mouth free of perversity; and keep corrupt talk far from their lips."* Proverbs 4:24. Plus, if the person we are trying to help is becoming combative, destructive or totally rejecting what we have to offer, we may have to step back until that person wants help.

The biggest contributor of negativity in a home or a relationship is when an individual violates the privacy of someone without their consent. There are many different reasons why our privacy could be violated; however, I will discuss a few. The most obvious reasons, on behalf of the violator will be due to insecurity, lack of trust, or suspicion; but, before I go any further, I must say that any parent that has a child under the age of 18, living at home must understand that their child has limited privacy. We are held accountable for our children, and it's imperative that we know them from the inside out—if we do not know our child's favorite color, their likes/dislikes, what motivates them, what discourages them, their dreams, their goals, what hurts them, or what they truly want to become when they grow up, then we are giving them too much privacy.

Now, if we violate the privacy of those who are not our children, we are out of order! If we are not getting paid to investigate, snoop, or pry into the lives of others, we should exercise extreme caution when doing so. Snooping, prying, or following someone, violates trust, and violated trust creates undue tension in a relationship, as well as undue emotional turmoil. In my opinion, the same drive that nudges an individual to try to get the 4-1-1 on or about someone will be the same information that could lead to us making that 9-1-1 call—to rectify the chaos or confusion that we may have brought to our own house. In my opinion, when we lack the understanding of someone, or when we look for dirt on someone to eventually throw mud, we will find that the residue of mudslinging will always leave its mark on our hands.

When we find ourselves going against the grain with someone about something that will benefit them in the long-run, it is possible that they do not want help, because his or her desires are elsewhere. When a person doesn't appreciate us or what we have to offer, we must find a way to move on to those who need us, opposed to fighting a losing battle. We cannot make a person want something or someone that they are not ready for. As a positive individual, it is imperative that we understand that we cannot change what people are accustomed to, nor compromise our integrity by getting upset with people who do not understand the benefits of having a positive attitude.

An individual who takes pride in what enters his or her eye gates and ear gates, by refusing to wallow in the folly of others, does not make an individual a negative person, it makes them WISE! [She] Wisdom has always revealed to me that God helps those who have a desire to help themselves; and, He also helps those who do not understand what they need as well, because scripture says, *"that you may be sons of your Father in heaven; for He makes His sun rise on the evil and on the good, and sends rain on the just and on the unjust."* Matthew 5:45. Although we may take a step back from them, God's grace and mercy will never change—it's here to stay, simply hope for the best, while allowing God to do the rest. At this point, we are able to free ourselves to allow the guided conscience to take over.

For the takeover to become effective, we must definitely understand that living a life permeated by negativity will lead to becoming consumed by the Spirit of Complaining. I have found that once an individual becomes accustomed to complaining, they will begin to give little thought to what they are doing. In so many words, complaining become second-nature, and the last thing we would ever want to do is insult a person's intelligence or kind-heartedness by an unjustified or unwarranted complaint. [She] Wisdom says that this is one of the biggest deal breakers known to man, and it will change the rules at any point in the game. For this reason, we must become ever so careful about our complaints; we do not want to become like the Children of Israel who wandered in the wilderness for 40 years due to their continuous complaints about everything. Nevertheless, the Children of Israel are the ones who left behind the *Eleventh Secret of Proverbs,* which is that [She] Wisdom will always step in to offer her assistance when we replace our Spirit of Complaining with the Spirit of Gratefulness.

Ungratefulness, or that nothing is ever good enough attitude is the type of attitude that will keep our blessings eluding us every time we turn around. As a matter of fact, if we see ourselves taking one step forward and two steps back, that's an indication that we must check our level of gratefulness. We need to check whether we are going in the wrong direction, whether we involve ourselves in the wrong things, or whether we are hanging around the wrong people, etc. Once we turn our ungratefulness into an ongoing state of appreciation, we will find that our lives will do an about-face, and our conscience will begin to open up in ways that would not open otherwise.

When we allow our conscience to become our guide, we will find that our conscience will not miss a beat—our conscience will free us, and it will ultimately convict us when needed. Although our conscience can be sifted based upon our environment, conditioning, or the lack thereof; however, we all know the difference between right and wrong, good and bad, as well as the positive and the negative, even if we pretend as if we do not know the difference. Now, if we run into someone who appears not to have a conscience, **RUN**— there is a problem from within! [She] Wisdom says, *"A prudent man sees evil and hides himself, the naive proceed and pay the penalty."* Proverbs 27:12. If our conscience doesn't convict us of our wrongdoings, misbehavior, betrayals or deception, we will find that the ones closest to us will begin to lose trust in us, or we will begin to accuse others of the same things that we are secretly guilty of. Believe it or not, our conscience and the conscience of others will reveal our true character through our actions, our reactions, our responses, and our spoken words. For me, I consider the conscience to be the "Writing on the Wall" of what's to come—all we need to do is take the time to read what it is saying, and not change it based on how we are feeling or what we want it to say.

Today, look for the good in others in all that you do, regardless of how it may appear while exercising the Power of forgiveness.

CHAPTER 10

The Power of Forgiveness

Why do we need to forgive someone who is constantly making a fool out of us? Forgiveness is a must in order for us to move on mentally, emotionally, and spiritually. We do not forgive someone for their sake; we forgive them for our own sake! So, what if we feel like a fool for forgiving? In my opinion, what makes us more of a fool is when we give someone power over our lives by controlling us when we have the power to disengage. Why would we want to torture ourselves when it's obvious that the person that we are holding a grudge against is living happily ever after or doing their own thing; and, we are torturing ourselves in our own emotions or allowing them to get in our head? Come on; it is not wise to cause ourselves to suffer when we have the option to live in freedom if we simply forgive and let go. When we hit the RESET button on our emotions making a choice to forgive, we are better able to glean from the vestibule of grace and mercy when it's our turn to be forgiven.

It is not a matter of IF we need forgiveness; it's a matter of WHEN. We are all a work in progress, regardless of how well we paint the picture; therefore, we must exercise our God-given right to forgive to ensure that when we fall short, grace and mercy becomes a shield to cover us even when we cannot foresee the wiles of the enemy. I am not saying that we will not get angry, but *"Be angry, yet do not sin. Do not let the sun set while you are still angry,"* according to Ephesians 4:26. If we need to vent, go ahead and do so; but, by the time the sun sets in the west, so should our anger. And, forgiveness should reside in our heart before we go to bed to ensure that we are able to have peace while we are sleeping. Unforgiveness is the main contributor to what we call insomnia; therefore, we must cleanse our soul of this negative emotion as soon as possible.

Do I have my moments? Absolutely! There are times when I just want to stay mad, especially when my kindness is taken as a weakness; but, I have trained myself so well until I cannot stay mad for long, even if I tried. I will forget about being mad, because my mind will automatically move on to a happy state superseding my emotions. Once the Spirit of Forgiveness becomes a part of who we are, grudges are less likely to be held against someone, unless there has been a severe psychological trauma that would cause that individual to temporarily harbor unforgiveness. However, in order to move beyond any type of trauma, forgiveness must take place whether it's a part of our character or not.

It's okay to hit that reset button on your emotions, on your forgiveness, or your favor, it is a gift that can be utilized at any given moment. [She] Wisdom says that it's imperative that you forgive those who have trespassed against you to ensure that you are able to be forgiven.

I am always bombarded with the question, "Why do bad things happen to good people?" In my opinion, it is the good and the bad that makes the world go round. In the midst of the good and bad, the positive and negative, as well as the right and wrong, we must *"Watch over our heart with all diligence, for from it flows the springs of life."* Proverbs 4:23. [She] Wisdom says that our issues are a silent representative of what is positively or negatively going on inside of us.

We will find that as the cycle of life continues, things will go right to go wrong, and things go wrong to go right according to the Biblical Law of seed, time, and harvest. There is good and bad in everyone; therefore, we must approach that question, "Why do bad things happen to good people?" as an eye-opener, lesson or distraction. [She] Wisdom says that *"In the house of the righteous there is much treasure, but in the revenue of the wicked is trouble."* Proverbs 15:6. We have to take into account whether our actions, reactions, or decisions are bringing about peace or chaos in our lives as well. Furthermore, we must remember that every person appears to be right in his or her own eyes, for *"The first one to plead his cause seems right, until his neighbor comes and examines him."* Proverbs 18:17. Therefore, self-examination is a must when asking the "Why?" questions, to ensure that we are looking from within self-first, and then looking outside of ourselves for answers. However, when doing so, just remember that as long as we have breath in our body, we are blessed. Yes, blessed to have an opportunity to turn a bad situation into a good one; besides, we would be surprised what someone would give to be where we are right now. In all that we do, look for the good, and do not allow a bad situation, circumstance, or event to cause us to forget about all the blessings that we have in and around us. More importantly, "Don't give up!"

Most often, when things are at their worst, that's when our blessing is right around the corner. The chaotic people, circumstances, or events are distractions to keep us from realizing our true blessing. Of course, we may have to let go of certain people, places, and things during our time of trial & tribulation; but, we must not give up on ourselves. For example, to find the most precious commodities such as gold, diamonds, rubies, or oil, we must dig deep into the earth to find them. God doesn't make a true blessing easy to come by; we must work for it. If our hands begin to feel as if they are slipping, hold on just a little longer—God is working it out. [She] Wisdom reveals that the *Twelfth Secret of Proverbs* is to simply dig deep, the oil, diamond, gold, and her rubies are waiting to be found within the depths of our very own soul. Not only that, [She] Wisdom also gave way to the *Thirteenth Secret of Proverbs* saying that smiling and laughing keeps our blood from boiling over with the atrocities of life.

What can a smile do for us, when we have nothing to smile about? I would definitely say that a smile can do more for us than a frown ever will. I have found that it's hard for me to stay mad or sad, when I have a smile on my face or when I laugh. As a matter of fact, a simple smile can brighten someone's darkest days if they allow it to do so; however, I have also found that laughter releases endorphins, strengthens our heart and relieves us of stress. If we pay attention, we will find that a smile will come automatically when we laugh, but when we simply smile, a laugh does not come automatically; therefore, making laughter more powerful. I am not saying to mock or pick on others for the sake of laughing, all I am saying is that if we allow laughter to become our therapy, it will bring healing and joy to our weary hearts while putting a smile on our face. As Proverbs 17:22 says, *"A joyful heart is good medicine, but a crushed spirit dries up the bones."* In my opinion, families, friendships, or relationships that laugh and pray together, stay together longer than the ones that do not. Besides, if we find a way to incorporate laughter into our day, we can never use the excuse that we have nothing to smile about—even when the vultures want to prey on our vulnerability, or do not appreciate who we are.

Appreciation has been designed to take us where criticism will not; and the moment we think that we have the upperhand in a situation or circumstance, without appreciation, it has the potential to go south on us. In all reality, we take the risk all the time, hoping that we can get and keep the people, places and things that we want without appreciating them; but, we are only buying time that will eventually run out. Believe it or not, when we allow appreciation to surface from within our very own soul through giving it, it brings about healing to the known or unknown wounded places that are buried within the depths of our soul. Keep in mind this scripture: *"for it is God who works in you both to will and to do for His good pleasure. Do all things without complaining and disputing, that you may become blameless and harmless, children of God without fault in the midst of a crooked and perverse generation, among whom you shine as lights in the world,"* Philippians 2:13-15. My little secret is whenever I am in doubt about anything, I give it to God whole-heartedly in the Name of Jesus, line it up with the Book of Proverbs, and then call forth [She] Wisdom, while using the *Book of Psalms* to pray about it. Therefore, if "IT," whatever that "IT" is, if it is not in the Will of God, He will shut it down or work it out for my good, guaranteed! If He does it for me, He will do it for anyone as long as their attitude is lining up according to His scripture. Not only that, if we take a moment to *Unriddle the Book of Proverbs*, it will also give us a better understanding of why bad things happen to good people and why good things happen to bad people. Could it possibly be linked to our composure?

CHAPTER 11

Keeping Our Composure

How do we keep our composure in an out of control world? In order to keep our composure, we must develop and nurture the control of self. In my opinion, everyone thinks that they have self-control, and they are correct to a certain extent; however, if the actions, reactions, and the attitude of what we consider to be our form of self-control are bringing about negativity, violating the will of others, or causing harm to ourselves or others, one must wonder is it really **SELF** that has control over us.

Our behavior and what comes out of our mouth reveals the contents of our heart, regardless of how hard we try to cover it up; therefore, giving birth to self-deception, allowing us to criticize or belittle others for the same things that we are guilty of. If this type of deception is not corrected, we unawaringly cause certain behaviors, practices, or characteristics to hover over our home to affect the weakest link; and most often, it is our children. If we look around, we will find that we must take a different approach to understanding and change our behavior, attitude, and mindset that are focused inwardly first, and then permeating as a ray of love, hope, and peace outwardly. Once we can do that, then the Power of Prayer will make the appropriate corrections necessary with the people, places, and things we come in contact with on a daily basis.

When we activate and understand self-control with the foundation of prayer, we have a little more stability to walk in faith with what we believe, not just by what we are taught or conditioned to think. The Power of our Instincts are attached to the Power of our Self-Control, and they will both grant us wisdom; however, if we want one without the other, we will find that they will cause a spiritual imbalance within the depths of our soul due to the lack of understanding between the two. How do we get the two to meet up? Great question! I am going to reveal another **Spiritual Secret**—the way in which to get our self-control to meet up with our instincts, we must **FAST**.

The Power of Fasting is the **ONLY** way to make our instincts meet up with our self-control, chasing the spirit of deception out of our loins to make the appropriate spiritual connections. *"But I keep under my body, and bring it into subjection: lest that by any means, when I have preached to others, I myself should be a castaway."* 1 Corinthians 9:27. Because, as Jesus clearly states in Mark 9:29, *"This kind can come forth by nothing, but by prayer and fasting."* If no one tells us, I will say it! **FASTING** has more power than we care to imagine as long as we do not use it to violate the will of another person. When we use it to empower ourselves, we gain the power over our flesh, we gain the power over our mind, we gain the power over our emotions, we gain the power over out of control situations, circumstances, and events that are beyond our control, and it gives us the power to rout demons in spiritual warfare.

Our faith is under attack, and if we do not get a grip and clear up this misunderstanding, we are going to become consumed by this **MIND CONTROL GERM** that has been planted in our community to break us as a nation. We do not need more violence; we need more people who are willing to **FAST** this nation through these atrocities to put self-control back into its proper perspective. It does not matter who gets the credit for this; I need you to do your part in sowing love, joy, peace, kindness, goodness, faithfulness, gentleness, self-control, fasting, and spreading this word of hope.

The *Book of Proverbs* is designed to empower, educate, and provide wisdom to all who partake of her—her meaning, [She] Wisdom! We can get into all types of fancy religions, and denominations to justify scripture, procedure, and proper protocol if we would like; but, for [She] Wisdom it's not necessary. It's clean cut and to the point for those who have a willing ear to hear. [She] Wisdom makes herself known in the *Book of Proverbs*; but, she does hide the wisdom in plain sight. However, she does give clues to what's important by repeating it several times or making a direct statement about what she hates or what is an abomination. For example: *"These six things doth the LORD hate: yea, seven are an abomination unto him: A proud look, a lying tongue, and hands that shed innocent blood, a heart that deviseth wicked imaginations, feet that be swift in running to mischief, a false witness that speaketh lies, and he that soweth discord among brethren."* Proverbs 6:16-19. Although, I used this scripture as an example, [She] Wisdom uses it as a guideline to reflect all the teachings and instructions of the seven abominations, or better yet, the seven character flaws that will keep our *Tree of Life* from bearing fruit. Here are the seven character flaws in my own words:

1. A proud look, prideful, or an arrogant person.
2. A lying tongue, gossiper, or a cheat.
3. Hands that shed innocent blood.
4. A heart that devises wicked plots.
5. Feet that are swift to run into mischief or to start trouble.
6. A deceitful witness that tell lies.
7. Him that soweth discord among brethren causing chaos and confusion.

[She] Wisdom states that the *Fourteenth Secret of Proverbs* is that the seven character flaws create a spiritual detachment, which inhibits the nocturnal Power of God to flow properly when our bodies are rejuvenating; therefore, causing a diurnal blockage that further contributes to our sinful nature. Let me break that down to give one a better understanding—the seven character flaws simply create a DISCONNECT from within the depths of our soul. It creates that emptiness or longing that keeps our body from properly recharging when we are sleep or it keeps us from sleeping period; therefore, affecting our Spiritual Alertness; or better yet, our INSTINCTS. Although, there are many other do's and do not's in the Bible, our character, our attitude, the way in which we communicate, and the way we treat others are of great importance according to [She] Wisdom.

In today's time, getting over on those who are naive, polite, or the non-confrontational individuals has become a way of life for those with a desire to cheat, manipulate, hurt, use, abuse, or control others. However, when we find ourselves a little naive about certain people, places, and things, we must simply put on our thinking caps to think outside, around, and through the box. Personally, I have found that the easiest way for me to think outside, around, and through the box is through using my book entitled, "*The Ancient Wisdom of Psalms*" for prayer, and Proverbial Scriptures for understanding. By doing so, it ensures that [She] Wisdom will provide the information needed to get me through whatever it is that I am dealing with or going through; therefore, all things work together for my good.

As life may have it, some people will pray about people, places, and things in their lives, and others will PREY on people, places, and things. It doesn't matter how strong we may appear, we all have weak spots—some more than others, but we all have them. Now, the difference in the ones who appear strong, they learn how to cover up their weaknesses, or they learn how to work through them. On the other hand, we have those who simply do not care about their weak spots; they let everything hang out, and they do not care about who or what their weaknesses are affecting. Just remember that an unresolved or overlooked weak spot will always bring its cousin déjà vu along, so beware. In so many words, if history keeps repeating itself regarding a situation, circumstance, or event—it's time to take a look from within. In my opinion, vultures can spot our weaknesses a mile away; and, that is exactly why they wait around to PREY on the weak, the naive, the sheltered, the ones who are not street smart/street savvy, and the ones that are blind to their own reality. Consequently, it is this type of unchecked or unrealized behavior that contributes to the long list of mental, physical, emotional, spiritual, and occasional abuse, even if we don't like to admit it. The answer to all of our questions lies within our very own soul—everything we need is within our reach, we must stretch ourselves, and with a great attitude when the timing is right, we will find the hidden treasures that we are looking for.

Having a positive mental attitude does not make us stupid, it enables us to allow our mind and our prayers to speak louder than our mouth when faced with a situation or circumstance that wants to prey on our vulnerability. There are times when we all feel as if we are on a winning or losing streak; however, we must understand that there will be times when we lose to win and win to lose. For me, when I lose, I consider it my pruning season with an understanding that no good thing will be withheld from me, because my **BLESSING** is waiting. When we believe that we are a winner from within, we become a magnet to winning, or if we think that we are a loser from within, we become that. For that reason, we must safeguard our mind to ensure that we do not fall by the wayside with wayward thinking or unjustified feelings of being used, misused, or abused.

If we find ourselves feeling used, misused or abused, then we must find a way to distance ourselves from the people that are causing it. [She] Wisdom says that it's *"Better is a little with the fear of the Lord, than great treasure and turmoil with it. Better is a dish of vegetables where love is, than a fattened ox and hatred with it."* Proverbs 15:16-17. However, to top it off, [She] Wisdom also says that the key word here is "feeling"—just because we feel a certain way, does not necessarily mean that it is the intent of that person; therefore, clarification of the intent is a must. Now, on the other hand, if we are conditioned to treat people a certain way, it is possible that people are treating us the same way we are treating them. This mirroring effect or pattern of how we treat people will continue in our lives unless we make a conscious effort to make a change. If a change is not made, the domino effects of feeling used, misused, or abused will continue to play itself out in the sensitive areas of our lives.

I firmly believe that self-analysis is important when developing a positive mental attitude regarding the way in which we are feeling. Now, if a person is making us feel a certain way, all we need to do is simply check to see how we are making them feel. If everything is copasetic on our end, we must then get clarification on their end to resolve or put to rest how we are feeling. If for some odd reason, they choose not to resolve the issue—please allow it to remain their problem, while releasing all attachments to it. I have found when our heart is broken over issues as such; that's more of a reason to listen to it. Our heart will tell us things that our emotions override based on our sense of vulnerability. Once we can get our emotions in check, we are then able to hear what our heart is saying—until then, we will find ourselves wallowing in things that our heart is trying to heal from. If we take the time to put our emotions on the backburner, we are then able to allow our heart to heal as we are pushed out of our comfort zone to understand the Matters of the Heart.

CHAPTER 12

The Matters of the Heart

The best way to evaluate whether or not our heart is in the right place is to check our motives. Our motives will reveal what the heart conceals—although, we play cat and mouse games when it comes down to being true to thyself; however, our actions, reactions, and what comes out of our mouth will reveal the contents of our heart in due time. What I have found is that when we are faced with a challenging battle of the heart, it is imperative that we sit down and make a list of the pros and cons regarding our motives. This will help draw out any form of deception—plus, if we lie to ourselves, who are we really cheating?

If we are doing anything out of jealousy, envy, strife, greed, revenge, anger, unforgiveness, or spite, that's an automatic sign that our heart is in the wrong place; and, we need to take it to God in prayer. Doing the right thing for the wrong reason is just as bad as doing the wrong thing for the right reason. We need to bring our heart and mind into a positive balance with each other to prevent bad karma from showing up when we least expect it. When our heart is in the right place, it gives us confidence in knowing who we are and what we stand for. Does this mean that we are perfect? Absolutely not, we are all a work in progress, but when we have a good heart, integrity is made evident in all that we do, say, and become. I will release a little secret, when we are able to govern our heart, which means to become a good steward over our heart, we are better able to control self. Self-control has a lot to do with the heart of man, and if we are able to understand how the two work hand-in-hand, we can become a master over our Mind, Body, Soul, and Spirit. If one has the desire for WISDOM, I am giving them the hidden secrets on a silver platter—this is indeed how I have received the wisdom that I possess today. Oh, by the way, [She] Wisdom says that we have a smorgasbord of wisdom buried within us that will flow from the depths of our soul if we do not allow folly to block our mental, emotional, or spiritual gateways.

Whatever we do in life, there will be a little give and take, ups and downs, positives and negatives, or setups and setbacks; but, this is where the *Book of Proverbs* comes in to help us bring balance to our lives, getting us out of our comfort zones. Actually, comfort zones are designed to be a temporary place, condition, or status. However, we are not designed to stay in one place; if we are comfortable with what we are doing that means that growth is not taking place in our lives. Wherever there is a lack of growth, we will find that we will naturally become a sluggard in that particular area if left unchecked; therefore, creating a comfort zone attracting the people, places, and things that contribute to that zone of choice.

[She] Wisdom says that if we depend upon being told what to do before we do it, we are already defeated. [She] Wisdom also reveals the *Fifteenth Secret of Proverbs* by saying that we must take authority, becoming proactive and diligent in all that we do, say, and become. Humbly thinking ahead and doing what it takes to get the job done, getting a situation taken care of, or bringing some sort of resolve are PRIMAL; therefore, keeping us in a class all by ourselves. This is what Proverbs 6:6-8 says to us, *"Go to the ant, you sluggard; consider its ways and be wise! It has no commander, no overseer or ruler, yet it stores its provisions in summer and gathers its food at harvest.* When we become codependent on others to tell us what, when, how, where, and why to do what needs to be done—we set ourselves up to become sluggards to life. Of course, sluggards are really easy to find because they are lazy, they sleep too much, they slouch on the couch all the time watching television, they lack the enthusiasm for life, they like to be served, they hate doing any form of work, they are untidy in their surroundings, they make excuses for their behavior, and most of all, they lack wisdom in the everyday decision-making process. However, this is what Proverbs 6:10-11says about the expected end of a sluggard, *"A little sleep, a little slumber, a little folding of the hands to rest"-- and your poverty will come in like a vagabond, and your need like an armed man.* As I have taken it upon myself to watch a colony of ants, I was really amazed. I actually destroyed their mound on purpose to see what they would do—they scattered, and by the next day, the mound was rebuilt bigger than the one I destroyed, along with an additional one. They did not settle for defeat, they just became proactive and diligent, becoming better than they were before while minding their own business. However, [She] Wisdom gave me the *Sixteenth Secret of Proverbs* from that colony of ants. [She] Wisdom points out that we are designed to serve others more than we are to be served. A humble servant is to be desired more so than a proud, arrogant person who tries to make slaves out of others.

Our lives cannot be a one-way street—it is designed to provide a benefit to the giver and the taker; therefore, creating a win-win situation. In so many words, to get what we want, we must give people what they want. If this is not the case, and we are always on the take, then we need to reevaluate our comfort zone before the Law of Karma catches up with us. Also, there are times when God blocks people from helping us, to push us out of our comfort zone, or to simply stretch us. In my opinion, it is better to adjust our thoughts and prayers to incorporate helping oneself to learn how to fish in that particular area of need, instead of being given a fish to provide temporary satisfaction. In so many words, it is better to learn how to acquire what's needed to help ourselves, opposed to being given something without learning what it takes to get it on our own. Of course, we all need a little help at some point; however, don't forget to learn the lessons that come with learning how to fish for the substance of our own to eliminate the status of codependency. Besides, depending on others to do what we are not willing to do for ourselves gives them the power to control that in which we relinquish our power to. So, our best bet is to come out of our comfort zone to think inside, outside, and around the box, while grabbing hold of our own sense of enthusiasm as an interdependent team player.

Enthusiasm is one of the easiest ways to begin to attract the people, places and things that we desire. Unfortunately, the lack of enthusiasm has a way of bringing about discontentment, complaining, and hatefulness that causes the desires of our heart to elude us. For example, if we are not enthused about our mate, our relationship will become strained; therefore, leaving room for someone else to capture his or her attention. If we are not enthused about our job, we will tend to make unnecessary mistakes, or create a hostile environment for others. I can come up with all types of examples; however, it doesn't make a difference what I say if we are grumpy about life in itself; besides, who wants to be with or live with a person who makes his or her life miserable. As the Book of Proverbs 21:9 tells us, *"It is better to dwell in a corner of the housetop, than with a brawling woman in a wide house."* In my opinion, whatever we are not enthused about will begin to lose its value as time passes on and the newness wears off; and, by that time, material gain will not compare to a peace of mind. For that reason, [She] Wisdom encourages us to stop bickering and complaining about life when the answers are already within.

The Wisdom of God has by far trumped anything that my mind can conceive—He is always blessing me to be a blessing to others. Trust me when I say that He will do the same for you as well. Therefore, work on getting your heart in the right place, and watch how God supernaturally pump wisdom through your veins when you least expect it, giving you the power to win in the midst of failure.

CHAPTER 13

The Power of Winning

In order to win, we must have the desire to do so; and, we must also have our gratefulness intact as well. If we are not grateful for our successes in life, they will appear as failures due to our mindset. It is imperative that we have a winning attitude in the midst of what appears to be a loss as well, because there are times when we will not win physically; but, we must win mentally and emotionally to ensure that we are able to create a win-win situation in order to make the appropriate corrections necessary. In my opinion, becoming a loser or winner is basically a mindset—we will win to lose and lose to win to complete the cycle of learning. It is indeed through the process of learning and understanding that we become WISE.

I will also say this, "It is okay to lose something or someone that's not good for us, or that will drain the life out of us." We cannot win all the time, and we will not lose all the time; however, if we believe that we are a winner at heart, and we perfect the skills of a winner, we will definitely win at more things than we will lose. We attract what we think about all the time, but winning is also a developmental process as well. We cannot sit around talking the game of a winner and not produce the result of a winner. We must work on ourselves every day, set goals, and work toward an end result of winning instead of living our lives like playing lotto or the luck of the draw, expecting great things to happen—real winning does not work like that!

Throughout my journey, I have found that winning is comprised of diligence, humility, compassion, and integrity; and, without it, one must question his or her MOTIVE for the appearance of superficial winning! Manipulating, conniving, scheming, and using people to get what we want are qualities that are NOT conducive to building lasting POWER of a truly winning personality. This type of individual quickly breaks the bonds of trust when they are on the losing end; therefore, we must exercise extreme caution when dealing with a person possessing this type of personality.

We need an awareness of why we are winning, we need an understanding of what it's going to take to win, we must be willing to do everything in the Spirit of Excellence, we need the motivation to win, especially when we want to give up, and we must be willing to pray while trusting the gift from within to supply all our needs. Real winners will not brag about being a winner, they simply get down to business and make things happen to create a win-win situation out of everything, without settling for defeat from the naysayers who are stuck on negative, stuck on material gain, or stuck on pimping them out to break their focus. It takes Y.O.U. to win—it is just a thought away, so create a win-win situation out of a negative one and don't be afraid to let go of what or who is not drawing out the winner inside of you.

Is timing really everything? The answer is yes—our timing means more than we care to imagine. Everything that we do, say, or become is based upon our timing. As we face the reality of living life, we may feel as if God is not making a way for our wants, needs, and desires; but in all actuality, He is. He knows what's best for us, and when the time is right He will answer us with a yes, no, or wait. Even with Abraham, he tried to force God's hand in having a male child when he had Ishmael with his maidservant. And, this goes to show that we cannot make God bless us—we can only prepare ourselves to be blessed through our actions, reactions, and thoughts. However, when the timing was right, God did indeed bless Abraham with Isaac, the Promised Son.

There are times when we cannot see what's ahead of us, and through God's grace and mercy, He carries us through. If we take a moment to look back over our lives, we will see how things somehow worked out for our good—although it may have been painful or difficult at the time, He worked it out for us. I must say that faith is the one thing that will carry us through even if the desire to give up comes into play. Trust me, it's the fear of the unknown that causes us to stress out, or feel hopeless when we don't know what's going to happen next. Believe it or not, we all feel that way at times; however, if we feel like that all the time—there is a problem.

We all have the same amount of time in a day—some people accomplish more than others because they have learned how to manage their time wisely. To save time, it is imperative that we plan to do so; if not, we will waste time doing unnecessary things that feed into our unproductivity. When we misappropriate our time, we will experience a higher level of stress, extreme fatigue, disrupted time with family, strained relationships, and/or a constant bout with failure. In my opinion, time is of the essence; therefore, it must be managed in order to maximize it, or we will not get anything done. For me, I simply determine the when, where, how, and why's of what's important by making a physical or mental list, and determine in advance what needs to get done first, and what can be dropped. Once I begin my day, I limit the amount of distractions that I will allow into my space to ensure that I do not waste time, or break my flow with people, places, and things that will take me in a direction that is not conducive.

I am not saying that we will not have distractions, because we will—our best bet is to train our minds in advance to deal with the distractions; therefore, we are better able to deal with the biggest time-wasters such as chatting on the phone, gossiping, texting, watching too much television, gaming, FaceBooking, etc. I have found through my own personal experiences that the difference between an effective or ineffective person is TIME MANAGEMENT. When we are busy accomplishing nothing is a big slap in the face, especially if we have nothing to show for it.

[She] Wisdom says that time is on your side, and it's waiting for you to decide how to manage it. If not, it will beyond a shadow of a doubt begin to manage you—dictating your life, pulling your strings, and stealing the true value of your time, while your blessings pass you by. [She] Wisdom also says that what God has for you is not going to come to you by luck, it's going to come to you by skill! So, when the timing is right, you don't want to be unprepared. The *Seventeenth Secret of Proverbs* is to prepare to succeed in that which you have not yet mastered, by diligently working to ensure that your seed, time, and harvest phase will bear good fruit when the time is right. For [She] Wisdom says that without a plan, you plan to fail by default. Today, make it your business to begin living, loving, learning, and understanding what it's going to take to get you to the next level to embrace the true greatness from within.

CHAPTER 14

Our Value

We are Abraham's seeds of greatness in the making—the only difference is that we have to begin to acknowledge that in which we are destined to become or accept who we are right now. The true greatness from within begins with our instincts—we were born out of instinct, so there is no reason to lose contact with the one thing that will let us know the truth, even when we are in denial about who we are, why we are, where we are, how we are, and what we are! As a matter of fact, according to the Bible, we are the Temple, even if we are not referred to as such. Although most may not agree with their body being a Temple, but our instincts will tell us otherwise if we dare to tap into the Hidden Wisdom that we possess from within.

[She] Wisdom has scriptures for both male and female; however, the male temptation from women has been the predominant concern from Abraham, David, King Solomon, and to the men of today's time. [She] Wisdom warns men the same way she warned King Solomon. We can spend years gaining the wisdom, mastering our lives, and lose it all in the end because of a woman. King Solomon was considered the WISEST MAN in his time, but in the end, he lost his kingdom because of women. Why? Was it because he became too arrogant? Was it because he had a void that he could not fill? Was it because he wasn't sexually satisfied? Was it because he followed his father King David's footsteps? Was it because of a generational curse? Or, was King Solomon just being a man? Well, the answer is that King Solomon was human just like we are; however, it was [She] Wisdom using Solomon to express herself, not the other way around. Although, God granted King Solomon **HER WISDOM**, He also stated that it was conditional. He said, *"So if you walk in My ways, to keep My statutes and My commandments, as your father David walked, then I will lengthen your days."* 1 Kings 3:14. However, King Solomon allowed his pride to get in the way, which is the number 1 thing that [She] Wisdom hates; as a result, it divided his kingdom.

[She] Wisdom is the *Tree of Life;* and, [She] Wisdom does not like to be mocked, period. The same standards that were held for King Solomon are held for us as well if we have a desire to partake of her. For the men, [She] Wisdom sends warning to us saying, *"Suddenly he follows her, as an ox goes to the slaughter, or as one in fetters to the discipline of a fool, until an arrow pierces through his liver; as a bird hastens to the snare, so he does not know that it will cost him his life."* Proverbs 7:22-23. For *"The one who commits adultery with a woman is lacking sense; He who would destroy himself does it. Wounds and disgrace he will find, and his reproach will not be blotted out."* Proverbs 6:32-33. [She] Wisdom wants to teach us how to deal with the impulsiveness and dangers associated with our ungoverned thoughts and actions. *"For it is written that "A wise man is cautious and turns away from evil, but a fool is arrogant and careless."* Proverbs 14:16. *"For her house sinks down to death, And her tracks lead to the dead; None who go to her return again, Nor do they reach the paths of life."* Proverbs 2:18-19. *"Lest strangers be filled with your strength, and your hard-earned goods go to the house of an alien; And you groan at your latter end, When your flesh and your body are consumed."* Proverbs 5:10-11. As [She] Wisdom would have it, in the latter days for a male, when he wears himself out sexually in his younger days, going from woman to woman, it is revealed that his sexual impotency will catch him in his latter days to consume his manhood; therefore, bringing about shame with the type of women that he has previously entertained. And, if he is lucky, maybe his Proverbs 31 woman is still waiting for him to regain his senses; or, maybe she will move on, who knows? But, what man would want to take that risk when the *Book of Proverbs* heeds such a warning.

Now, what I have found is that every woman wants to be that Proverbs 31 woman, but somehow doesn't understand that the Proverbs 31 woman is the last chapter of Proverbs. That means that in order to become that Proverbs 31 woman, we cannot bypass Proverbs 1-30. We must master the previous chapters first, and the Proverbs 31 woman is automatic—that is the true reward that [She] Wisdom gives to women who place her first. [She] Wisdom frowns upon a woman trying to reap the benefits where she has not sown. Ladies if we want what [She] Wisdom has to offer us, we must act like a real lady and not a thief; seducing, and manipulating men into wanting something that we have not mastered. *"For the lips of an adulteress drip honey and smoother than oil is her speech; but in the end she is bitter as wormwood, Sharp as a two-edged sword."* Proverbs 5:3-4. The way in which we communicate is a dead giveaway regarding our motives, and a woman with an uncontrollable mouth is a target for emotional turmoil, as well as a disruptive household. Do we think that [She] Wisdom will give us the ability to love others with conditions? Do you think [She] Wisdom will allow us to manipulate her prestige just to put on a show? Do we think that [She] Wisdom will prize us as a virtuous woman through flattery? The answer is NO! [She] Wisdom will only select those who are teachable, trainable, faithful, realistic, honest with themselves, and willing to embrace the Tree of Life, *for her price is far above rubies.*

I am not going to preach to the choir—I am just going to expose the things that are already inside of us. As we all instinctively know, our body is indeed our Temple; however, in my opinion, it is the most misused and abused part of God's creation. When we do not respect our Temple, we will find that after the thrill is gone in whatever we are doing, saying or becoming, utter chaos will secretly find its way into the depths of our soul. If that is hard to believe, then look at the divorce rate—80% of marriages are ending in divorce. Why? The reason is that we have become driven by power, money, and sex—not our instincts; therefore, leaving our very own soul with a longing that brings a force of negativity that craves chaos.

Let's dig a little deeper on the cravings of the power, money, and sex trance. In my opinion, when dealing with this type of power and money trance, if an individual has no power or status, or just simply broke—they become a slave to society, lacking the respect of those who have. In all reality, the ones that do not have, cannot become a part of the elite groups of people, until their income level changes, social status changes, or they become sexually controlled by the elite pimps. Now, as we deal with the sex trance at hand, if an individual does not have money or status, but is willing to use sex as a tool or weapon to obtain money, power, status, a dinner, a movie, or just to make ends meet, it is indeed a form of prostitution. I am not just talking about the prostitution that takes place on the street corners, I am referring to the undercover sex slaves that sit next to us on the job, in the church, in the pulpit, lives next door to us, or maybe lives in our own house with us—who knows, the list goes on!

Undercover sex slaves are not just limited to females—in today's time, men are selling out faster than females to get what they want. Although we do not like hearing the truth, it does not surprise me about what we will, or will not do behind closed doors! We are quick to judge others for selling their souls to the devil, sliding down a pole in the strip clubs, or selling/using drugs to name a few; but, when it comes down to power, money, or sex—we do not know what we would do until our back is up against the wall. Make no mistake about it, positively or negatively, everyone has a story, and everyone has a price! A price that they would pay, or a price they would not pay for power, money, or sex; as well as a story to justify the behavior. If our instincts are not in full working order, it's possible that we may fall short in this particular area.

I have found that there are two obvious signs that our soul is in utter chaos: 1. If we are a person who has everything, who is not happy, and is always on the take, while crucifying others for not living up to their expectation. 2. If we are a person who has nothing, who doesn't want anything and prides himself/herself on crucifying others for wanting more out of life; or better yet, a person who enjoys killing the dreams of others to keep them at their level or in a box. Nevertheless, I have also found that to maximize our understanding of the Temple from Within, we cannot allow outside appearances, circumstances, or events that are related to power, money, or sex to interfere with our instincts. Yes, I said INSTINCTS! This is one major element of who we are that gets ignored the most—we can instinctively do, create, and become if we simply allow our instincts to take its rightful place in our Temple. By doing so, it will allow joy, peace, patience, kindness, goodness, generosity, gentleness, faithfulness, modesty, and self-control to enter our lives to give us a conscience worth having.

[She] Wisdom says that our instincts and our conscience work together to guide and protect us. When they are not working together, it is possible that our conscience is convicting us of some form of guilt. Nevertheless, our instinctual nudges from within will speak louder than anyone we know, but we must listen to it carefully to filter out the negative self-talk. Our instincts are not negative in nature, so if negative things are being felt from within, or we feel compelled to do something negative—IT IS NOT OUR INSTINCTS! For me, along with my instincts, I use a scripture from the Bible that says "Be fruitful and multiply." It says to be fruitful and multiply, not be fruitful and divide— if things are dividing, it is for a reason, for a season, or for a lesson; and, we must prayerfully decide which one! We must pay attention to the things that appear to be going right, and understand what appears to be going wrong to ensure that the complexities of life do not overwhelm us with confusion.

Our greatest potentials in life are wrapped up in our attitude; it is the one thing that will measure that in which is immeasurable, as it creates a life of endless possibilities. Listen to me, if we have enough faith to allow a negative attitude to rule & reign in our lives, it is fair to say that we have enough faith to allow God to change our negative attitude into a positive one; besides, it takes the same amount of energy. The simplest way to develop confidence in our positive mental attitude is to believe in oneself, without becoming frustrated by the opinions of others. However, the lack of confidence will cause the best of us to use everything and everyone as an excuse of why we are not taking action, or why we are not succeeding in certain areas. From this point on, no more excuses!

As greatness begins to reveal itself, every challenge or limit will only present itself so that we can develop an action plan to work on them, or to work through them. By doing so, this will definitely enable us to turn our limitations and challenges into opportunities. I believe that there is no limit on what we can achieve when we are confident that we know our stuff. At the end of the day, there is no need to limit ourselves to something as simple as our attitude—make the change to a having a positive mental attitude about everything and everyone, while allowing our gift to make room for us. After completing this book, rest assured that disappointments will become minimized, to allow the fullness of life to illuminate the true greatness regardless of who likes or dislikes us.

From my perspective, if someone does not like us, that is their problem, not ours, unless we have given them a reason to dislike us. If someone does not get to know the true person that we are, then it's time to move on anyway. If we are doing the right thing by operating in outright integrity, we do not need to convince a person to like us, nor do we have to change who we are to fit into a particular circle just to become likable. It is imperative that we come into our own individuality; as long as we are not operating in waywardness to cause people to dislike us, then we have nothing to worry about.

In my opinion, it is only envy, jealousy, or hatefulness that would cause one to dislike those who they know nothing about. However, if we are exhibiting negative characteristics to offend, betray, or hurt innocent people, then one should have the option to dislike our behavior, attitude, action, or reaction. It does not matter what we do, say, or become, someone is not going to like it, or someone may have something to say about it, but we cannot allow it to stop us from becoming who God created us to be.

Our value does not reside in someone liking us; our value resides in us liking ourselves for who we are. When we lose value in ourselves, we will depend on others to value us instead; and, when that does not happen, we will feel as if we are unworthy of his or her love. In my opinion, that should not be the case, but it happens all too often. How do we know if we are valuable to someone? We will know if someone values us when we find value in ourselves first. If we do not find value in ourselves, we will not appreciate the fact that a person has found us to be valuable; therefore, we will become ungrateful, taking more than we are giving. This is exactly how people tend to get used and abused.

Most often, people will treat us based on how we see and treat ourselves, unless they are being vindictive trying to break down a person who takes pride in themselves. Nevertheless, we can spot those types of individuals by where they place their value; as a rule of thumb, what we find value in gets our love, time, money, priority, and other resources. If we pay closer attention to this, it will indeed safeguard one from a lot of deceptive people. What we value enables us to set priorities of what's important to us; but when our values are not in the right place, we will find that we will begin to make bad decisions, wrong decisions, or controlling decisions based upon where our heart is. Listen, where there is no value found in what we have to offer, we must find a way to get into an environment where our true value is found. In so many words, deal with people that bring out the best and not the worst—when we become better, and not bitter about how we live our lives, as well as how we see ourselves, our whole outlook on life will change to ensure that we are able to gain control over our lives.

CHAPTER 15

Controlling the Situation

How do we gain control of our lives without losing ourselves in the midst of change? The first step to gain control over our lives is to understand that we are not able to control everything. We cannot control others, nor should we violate their will—if we have not noticed by now, even God will not violate our will. He gives us options by allowing the issues of life to consume us; but the bottom line, we make our own choices. In my opinion, that is where gaining control over our lives begin—it is indeed with our choices. However, the moment that we think that we need to fix someone else, that is the moment that we need to take a look from within to fix self. We are not here to fix people; we are here to help, motivate, and encourage others—fixing people is God's job, not ours because we are all imperfect in some area of our lives. We as a people must recognize that we are a source of inspiration to someone, and it is through that disappointment that we unawaringly lead those who look up to us astray.

Nevertheless, it is our responsibility as a child of the Most High to lead without intentionally causing dismay to those who are counting on us to lead them. Every generation must become better than the previous one, and if we are digressing in that formality, we must gain control over our lives to leave a legacy worth leaving behind. We have not gone through all of our challenges for nothing; we have not overcome insurmountable defeat to allow it to go in vain—it is time to gird up our loins, get back on track, and live the life that God has predestined for us to live. Everything we need is already within us, every experience has provided a roadmap for us to follow, and all we need to do is become a master over our mind, instincts, emotions, and the divine wisdom from within.

Although we may not be able to explain a lot of things about our lives, what's taking place, or the reasons why; but if we can embrace or open ourselves up to the Wisdom of God, I promise that He will redefine everything about our mind, our emotions, and our instincts; therefore, giving us the ability to move into our faith and favor at the appropriate time. Let me say this, faith and favor without God will render one's mind scattered, emotions all over the place, and our instincts ineffective. In my opinion, if that is what's happening, it is better to use the tool that God has given us to gain our POWER back, and that is the power of PRAYER. [She] Wisdom says that all you have to do is stop trying to overcomplicate life, learn to live in peace, pray about everything, and embrace the Wisdom of God to govern your mind, your emotions, and your instincts. Once this is done, I promise you that the Mind, Body, Soul, and Spirit will make a true believer out of you, changing your whole outlook on life as long as you do not become a control freak!

How can we spot a control freak? There are times when it's obvious to spot a control freak, especially when they are trying to control, manipulate, and bribe others to do what they want to be done. However, there are silent control freaks that are not so apparent with his or her behavior, because they have learned how to conceal their behavior to get what they want, like a wolf in sheep's clothing.

Now, the question is, "How can we spot a wolf in sheep's clothing?" To detect this type of individual, one must open up their eye gates, ear gates, and instincts; and, if we are emotional, we may miss their cue! One must get out of his or her feelings, if they do not have a desire to become the next victim—exuding too many emotions when dealing with a control freak or a wolf in sheep's clothing, clouds our sense of judgment, while clueing them in on our weaknesses or our pressure points. In my opinion, there are a few signs that I look for to truly understand who or what I am dealing with— the first sign is out of control anger problems. It does not matter if they are nice to us right now, when this person does not get what they want or cannot control the situation, their niceness to us will be out the window. And, we will see them for who they really are; hopefully, by that time, it's not too late. The second sign, we must pay attention to how they are treating other people, because the same way that they treat others will be the same way that they will treat us when we get their timing wrong. The third sign, if this person is abusive verbally, mentally, physically, emotionally, or spiritually—BEWARE. These are tell-tale signs that this individual may have a problem with respecting others and that they may lack a conscience; therefore, it is imperative that one must tread with caution. If not, expect to become the next victim, because a control freak or the wolf in sheep's clothing is truly a victim who is recruiting or creating other victims to keep the cycle of human trauma, hurt, and destruction going to contribute to the mental and emotional anguish.

If you are the control freak or the wolf in sheep's clothing, there is hope for you. [She] Wisdom says that you have an opportunity to replace your negative characteristics with positive ones such as love, joy, peace, kindness, goodness, faithfulness, gentleness, and self-control. Remember, a good name is chosen—always elect to do the right thing, and watch how God will send blessings your way when you least expect it, regardless of what anyone thinks of you or says about you.

CHAPTER 16

The Ego Challenge

How do we overcome our egotistical behavior? Egos come and go—they are all around us and within us as well. Our ego contributes to our prideful, arrogant behavior that causes one to think that they are more than they are or better than certain people based on their power, money, sex, or status. If we pay close attention we will find that our ego has a way of causing us to build a hidden resistance to following instructions; it will also cause us to degrade those who appear not to be up to our standards or beneath us. A tell-tale sign of a super inflated or busted ego is when a person is driven to compete with others, compare themselves with others all the time, or wanting what others have in order to fit into a certain clique. Is it a bad thing? In my opinion, it really depends on who is looking or who we are hurting. The pride of life has been one of the greatest downfalls of man today; therefore, we must reverse the effect to ensure that we are able to build, mentor, and leave a legacy to empower generations to come, without dividing ourselves as well as the people around us.

Our ego is what places us in a box, and it also will cause us to place others in a box; when we should be empowering and releasing ourselves as well as others out of it. The way that I recognize a confident person is by looking for their humility. True confidence is expressed in our ability to be who we are without bragging or boasting about it, but simply being about it. Our mouth can say a lot of things, but if our actions or reactions are not lining up, then there is a disconnect somewhere; and we need to find it! A confident person will never have to say a word about his or her confidence. It's indeed a natural occurrence that radiates from within that's revealed in our ability to exhibit love, joy, peace, kindness, goodness, faithfulness, gentleness, and self-control without being told to do so or without giving it a second thought.

You cannot go wrong being humble; it is humility that opens the door to Divine Favor in places where the door was completely closed. Trust me, humility is indeed your trump card, especially when you are in need of something that you do not have already or when you have a true desire to "Do You."

CHAPTER 17

Our Setbacks Are A Setup!

Overcoming a setback has to become a mindset; if not, one will continue to live that setback over and over again without doing anything about it. In my opinion, setbacks are hidden lessons to bring us into the classroom of life. If we do not understand what God is trying to say to us, what God is trying to teach us, what direction God is trying to lead us in, what corrections that we need to make in our lives, or what has become god in our lives over Him, that lesson will continue to repeat itself until we get it. Therefore, there is no reason to blame anyone for our setbacks—it's never about them, it's always about us.

We have to look from within to find the lesson, and once we find the lesson, it is wrapped in Divine Wisdom. Listen to me, a setback for me is wisdom being handed to me on a silver platter—I eat it up, and I share it to activate the Law of Reciprocity. I was told some time ago that I need to break what I'm saying down so that a little child can understand— so, let me explain. When I am served a setback, obstacle, or difficult situation, I become a student, learning the lesson from it; and then, I turn around to become the teacher to empower others to open the floodgate of WISDOM. Seed, time, and harvest apply to our setbacks as well; and it cannot hold us back if we simply set it up to become a blessing for ourselves and others. If we can find a way to learn from our setbacks and create a win-win situation by looking for the positive without focusing on the negative, [She] Wisdom will be waiting to provide us with the substance or provisions needed to overcome the situation, circumstance, or event.

In my opinion, a setback is a distraction to keep us blind, confused, and frustrated with ourselves; nevertheless, when we exercise wisdom, compassion, and due diligence when dealing with a setback, we are better able to maneuver around obstacles to achieve our desired goals. Here is a prime example, if we crush an ant mound, we will never see them weeping or settling for defeat—they will rebuild that mound by any means necessary regardless of whether we want them there or not; it is sad to say, but it is only death that will stop an ant from rebuilding its empire.

If something or someone rains on our parade, simply dry off, regroup, get a strategy, and go for it again! A true winner will not stop because of a setback; they simply find another way. [She] Wisdom advises that we leave no stone unturned; regardless of how it may appear. Your best bet is to refrain from settling for defeat mentally, do what you have to do to overcome your setbacks emotionally, and keep yourself moving physically, to ensure that you do not have any regrets about giving up on YOU. Oh by the way, if you add a little prayer to it, you will indeed enhance your Spiritual Powerhouse causing the spirit of defeat to flee. Yes, prayer is like the icing on the cake that bridges the triumphant gap commencing all things to work together for your good to keep you out of those dry places.

A dry place or drought in life is a time of self-correction. In my opinion, a drought is nature's way of correcting itself to keep universal balance and harmony. This principle is applicable to every aspect of life; therefore, a drought does not enter our lives to kill us—it comes to heal us in places that we are knowingly or unknowingly wounded, handicapped, or disobedient. Of course, we are all a work in progress; however, when we stop progressing in the area of our purpose or when we become codependent, we will find that we will begin to thirst for something or someone that's not conducive to our wellbeing. When we quench our thirst with the wrong thing, it will keep us all over the place mentally and emotionally, it will keep us running to and fro in our busyness accomplishing nothing, or it will keep us wallowing in a bed of indecisiveness that will delay our bountiful harvest. Today, take the time to master those dry or thirsty places in your life to ensure that you do not defy the purpose of your drought and to ensure that you are able to live a good life.

CHAPTER 18

The Good Life

In order to live the good life so to speak, we have to choose it. As I have journeyed through life, I have found that we create the life that we desire to live mentally first, through our mindset. If we think that we have it made, we will! If we think that our lives are a living nightmare, then it will become just that! Rich or poor, successful or unsuccessful, college degree or no degree, we have a say so in whether we live a good life or a nightmare. We definitely become what we think about all the time, like attracts like, and the list goes on; however, it all boils down to our thought process and our perception; therefore, we cannot blame anyone for the end result of what takes place in our lives.

Bad things happen to good people, and good things happen to bad people; however, that does not mean that we cannot have a good life because things happen. Life is very fickle, but I will say this, if we think or say that we are a loser, our life will follow that pattern. Regardless of how much money we have, regardless of how many degrees we have, or regardless of who or what we have or know, we will subconsciously find a way to prove ourselves correct according to the thermostat that we have set in our mind. In so many words, our lives are forced to regulate to the condition of our mindset, even if we get lucky or get a big break in life.

The lottery is a prime example of this philosophy: a person can win millions of dollars, yet spend every dime of it within a few years, losing everything. Why? It is the mindset—we must change the way in which we think. Now, on the other side of this, we have someone that is rich, but they hoard every dime—they cannot live a fulfilled life because their mindset is stuck on who is trying to swindle money out of them. They have money, but they can't live a good life due to the fact that they think that everyone is up to no good. Living in fear of losing creates a Mind Germ within one's self that places this individual on a losing streak with people leaving them lonely and destitute from within.

In my opinion, if we can find a way to understand and own the fact that we are indeed a miracle, we will attract miracles. Once we develop that mindset, our lives will become surrounded by blessings and goodness that's beyond what we could have ever imagined. We are the life that keeps on giving, and if we are sharing goodness, living in goodness, and thinking good thoughts—the Law of Reciprocity has to bring it back into our lives. For example, if a man asks us for water, we must give him water out of the goodness of our heart, expecting nothing in return; therefore, goodness along with favor has to come back to us in our time of need. But, if a man asks for water and we laugh, giving him nothing when we are empowered to do so, or we give in vinegar for water, we have just caused the Law of Reciprocity to bring back in full-circle the seed that we have sown. Along with the mindset of goodness, our actions and reactions must become good as well—we cannot live by a double-standard of being good to certain people, and neglecting others. Just remember that sowing goodness is a prerequisite to continue living the good life; and, the moment we change our mind on goodness, it will withhold its reward. Living the good life is within your reach, and it is your responsibility to extract the good out of all that you do, say, and become.

CHAPTER 19

Where Did The Time Go?

Time management is the one thing that most of us take for granted. In my opinion, time is on our side, and if we give it the opportunity to serve us, it will provide us with enough time to get things done with time left over. When we rush, rush, rush, we cannot say that we accomplish more, but we can say that we make more mistakes when we do rush. If this is happening, this is where setting priorities come into play— I have found that creating a To-Do list really helps to keep us on track or to get back on track when necessary. We must be able to deal with change when our To-dos are disrupted, and we must be able to get back on track without allowing our emotions or our mind to become the Devil's playground. In so many words, we cannot overthink issues when our To-dos become little boo-boos! Safeguarding our mind is a prerequisite to gaining control over our time—we all have the same amount of time in the day, it's how we manage it that creates the lack or abundance.

How can we change our mindset toward time? I am so glad to answer that question! I have found that the best way to manage our time is to relax in it. If we find peace in the midst of our busyness, it will grant us the ability to think clearly, set priorities, and provide a way to manage our reactions or actions when we have a disruption. Most often, when we make others feel as if we are too busy for them, they subconsciously pull away; eventually causing a disconnect in the relationship. Even if we are busy, we must find a way to take a moment to give those we love our undivided attention; it only takes a fraction of a second to show an individual that they are more important than what really has our attention.

The mismanagement of time has caused more broken relationships than we would care to imagine—the truth is……..if social media is getting more time than our family or if social media is getting more time than the ones that truly have our back, then we must reevaluate the management of our time. Trust me, if there is something that we want to really do or someone that we really want to see, we will make time, by any means necessary. Excuses about not having enough time are just that, AN EXCUSE! Think About It!

If something or someone is not a part of our To-Dos, own it, and be so kindly to put it on the To-Don't list. You do not have to make an excuse for wasting time on people, places, and things that are not conducive to where you are going or what you want to do because folly is [She] Wisdom's least favorite characteristic.

CHAPTER 20

Folly at Its Best

Why do we do what we do? Or, better yet, why are we not doing what we should be doing? The why's of life gives us an opportunity to understand ourselves when we are misunderstood regarding what we are doing, saying, or becoming by simply asking fact-finding questions of purpose. When we take the time to understand the what's, when's, where's, how's, and why's of life, we then get the precious privilege of opening the gate to the Fountain of Wisdom that's buried within the depths of our very own soul. Yes, we have the answers within us, and all we have to do is seek the answers from within opposed to getting the superficial opinions from people who are not connected to our soul. I am not saying that receiving advice is wrong—I am saying that the advice that one receives from someone else should bring confirmation to the answers that we receive from within. Therefore, we have less time to focus on being judged or judging others on what we may be guilty of ourselves or what we have hidden in our past repertoire of secrets that are filed under a different label according to our level of blindness or our perception of our reality.

We have all done something that we are not proud of, and we will all fall short at some point in our lives. However, if we are always falling short or if we are always doing things that we are not proud of, then it is fair to say that is indeed recognition of foolish behavior. When we are doing things that will affect us, our family, or the innocent negatively or out of selfishness, we must question our reasons for such folly.

The Bible speaks of foolishness, folly, and waywardness time and time again; yet we continue to exhibit selfish behaviors to quench an inner thirst from within, not realizing that we will thirst again. The more we partake of foolishness, the more we will crave it; and, the more we crave it, the more we become engulfed in that type of behavior causing our conscience to take a back seat. In my opinion, an idle mind becomes the Devil's playground to overthink and create issues that are only real to the person that's allowing him to play! Once this happens, we can bank on folly seeping out of our loins even if we think that we are right in our own eyes. How do we know if it's happening to us? Mental exhaustion is the first sign, feeling stressed out is the second sign, and feeling depressed is the third sign—this type of violation will breakthrough when we are mentally, emotionally, physically, and spiritually weak. The best way to safeguard our mind or shut down the Devil's playground is to stay busy, pray, read the Bible, know how to apply the Scriptures to practical life, and create a win-win situation out of everything.

When our muscles are tense, so is our brain; therefore, breaking our flow. Once our flow is broken, we will find that everything will begin to hit us at once to shift our state of being. If we have a desire to maximize our full potential, we must give our bodies the opportunity to relax first, and then allow it to perform mentally, emotionally, physically, or spiritually. I am living proof, when we respect our bodies, it will respect us. This is your opportunity to shut down the Devil's playground mentally, emotionally, physically, and spiritually to safeguard your ability to think clearly, relax, and allow your creative juices to flow; therefore, creating a win-win situation out of yesterday's folly. [She] Wisdom says that it is your time to take a moment to look within for the answers to life most mind-boggling questions about why you are doing what you are doing or why you are not doing what you should be doing. WISDOM has finally come home to **ROOST**! Now that you have the Secrets to Wisdom—your Inner Wisdom awaits your quest for it.

{She} Wisdom

PROVERBIAL GUIDE

Proverbial Need	Proverbs
7 Abominations	6:16-19
A Child Left to Himself	29:15
A Good Name	27:21
A Lazy Man	26:13-16
A Soft Answer	15:1-2
Adultery	5:1-23
Adultery	6:20-29
Angry People	29:22
Answering a Fool	26:4-12
Anxiety	12:25
Bad Influences	28:10
Bearing False Witness	25:18
Becoming Proactive	10:4-5
Becoming Satisfied with Your Wife	5:15-19
Beginning of Wisdom	9:10-12
Being Hard-Headed	15:5
Benefits of Allowing Wisdom In	2:10-21
Benefits of Listening to Wisdom	1:33
Benefits of Wisdom	4:10-13
Beware of Angry People	22:24-25
Beware of Loose Women	23:26-28
Beware of Oaths	6:1-5
Beware of Wayward Men and Women	1:10-18
Bitterness	14:10

Deception vs. Righteousness	12:15-22
Deceptive Work vs. Righteous Work	11:18-21
Declaration of Wisdom	8:14-31
Depression	12:25
Direction from God	3:5-6
Dishonest Gains	13:11
Dishonesty	20:23
Dishonesty vs. The Just	11:1
Disobedience	15:5
Doing What's Rights	3:29-30
Driving Out Foolishness	22:15
Envy	3:31
Envy	14:30
Envy Withheld	23:17-18
Equally Yoked Friends	27:17
Excellent Wife	12:4
Favor	13:15
Favor of the Lord	12:2
Fear of the Lord	1:1-7
Fear of the Lord	15:16
Finding a Good Thing	18:22
Flee from Evil	27:12
Foolish Women	9:13-18
Friendliness	18:24
Gateway of Our Mouth	13:2-3
Generosity	22:9
Get Away from Evil	4:27
Get Up and Get Moving	6:6-11
Get Up Early in the Morning	20:13

Gift Making Room for You	18:16
Giving	3:9-10
Giving Praise	27:2
Good Charity	28:27
Good Name	22:1
Good Words vs. Bad Words	10:11
Gossip	26:20-22
Governing Our Mouth	18:4-8
Gracious Woman	11:16
Greed	13:25
Greedy Person	1:19
Guarding Our Mouth	21:23
Happiness	3:13-15
Hard-Headedness	29:1
Harlotry	7:6-27
Hate Instructions	12:1
Hatred vs. Love	10:12
Helping Others	3:27-28
Helping the Poor	21:13
Hidden Hatred	10:17
Hoarding	11:24-26
Holding Your Peace	11:12
Hope	13:12
How to Respond Appropriately	15:1-2
Humility	3:7-8
Humility	15:33
Humility	22:4
Hypocrites	11:9
Idleness	19:15

Listening to Wisdom	8:32-35
Lust of the Flesh	5:1-23
Merciful Debts	22:26-27
Merciful People	11:17
Mercy for the Needy	14:31
Miser	11:24-26
Mocking the Poor	17:5
Motivation	12:25
Need Understanding and Knowledge	1:1-7
Oppressing the Poor	14:31
Order of Wisdom	9:1-6
Overworking to Become Rich	23:4-5
Paying Attention to Life	4:20-27
Paying Attention to the Actions	14:15-19
People Pleasers	29:4
Perverse People	3:32
Perverseness	15:4
Plans of Action	16:9
Price of Wisdom	8:11
Pride	16:18-19
Pride & Arrogance	8:12-13
Pride vs. Humility	11:2
Pride vs. Humility	29:23
Providing Good-Ground	27:23-27
Prudent Man	22:3
Pure Heart	22:11
Quick-Tempered	14:29
Rape	6:32-33
Repercussions of Rejecting Wisdom	2:22

Proverbial Guide | Ruby Fleurcius

Train Up Your Child	22:6
Tree of Life	11:30
Tree of Life	13:12
Tree of Life	15:4
Trouble Maker	27:14
Trouble Makers	24:1-2
Trust in the Lord	29:25
Trusting God	3:1-35
Truthfulness	23:23-25
Unfair Business and Dealings	20:10
Value of Keep Your Lips	10:19-21
Value of Wisdom	3:13-18
Virtuous Woman	31:10-31
Walking with the Wise vs. Fools	13:20
Wayward Woman	5:1-14
Wayward Women	9:13-18
We Are Right in Our Own Eyes	21:2
What Comes Out of Our Mouth	8:5-11
What Wisdom Will Do for You	4:5-13
What You Need to Do for Wisdom	4:8-9
Where is Wisdom Found	10:13
Who House the Lord Blesses	3:33
Who is Wisdom & Understanding	7:4
Who Receives Grace	3:34
Who to Confide In	25:19
Who to Stay Away From	4:14-17
Who You Should Not Break Bread With	23:6-8
Wholesome Tongue	15:4
Wicked Intentions	12:2